卞尺丹几乙し丹卞と

Translated Language Learning

The Fisherman and his Soul

渔夫和他的灵魂

Oscar Wilde

English / 普通话

Copyright © 2023 Tranzlaty
All rights reserved.
Published by Tranzlaty
ISBN: 978-1-83566-051-5
Original text by Oscar Wilde
The Fisherman and his Soul
First published in English in 1891
www.tranzlaty.com

The Mermaid
美人鱼

Every evening the young Fisherman went out to sea
每天傍晚，年轻的渔夫都出海了
and the young Fisherman threw his nets into the water
年轻的渔夫把网扔进了水里
When the wind blew from the land he caught nothing
当风从陆地上吹来时，他什么也没抓到
or he caught just a few fish at best
或者他最多只钓了几条鱼
because it was a bitter and black-winged wind
因为那是一阵苦涩的黑翅膀风
rough waves rose up to meet the wind from the land
汹涌的海浪掀起，迎面而来的风
But at other times the wind blew to the shore
但在其他时候，风吹到岸边
and then the fishes came in from the deep
然后鱼从深处进来了
the fishes swam into the meshes of his nets
鱼儿游进了他的网里
and he took the fish to the market-place
他把鱼带到市场
and he sold all the fishes that he had caught
他把捕到的鱼都卖掉了

but there was one special evening
但有一个特别的夜晚
the Fisherman's net was heavier than normal
渔夫的网比平时重
he could hardly pull his net onto the boat
他几乎无法将网拉到船上
The Fisherman laughed to himself
渔夫自嘲地笑了起来
"Surely, I have caught all the fish that swim"
"当然，我已经钓到了所有游泳的鱼"

"or I have snared some horrible monster"
"或者我抓住了一些可怕的怪物"
"a monster that will be a marvel to men"
"一个对人类来说将是一个奇迹的怪物"
"or it will be a thing of horror"
"否则这将是一件可怕的事情"
"a beast that the great Queen will desire"
"伟大的女王会渴望的野兽"
With all his strength he tugged at the coarse ropes
他用尽全身力气拉扯着粗绳
he pulled until the long veins rose up on his arms
他拉扯着，直到长长的血管在他手臂上升起
like lines of blue enamel round a vase of bronze
就像青铜花瓶周围的蓝色珐琅线条
He tugged at the thin ropes of his nets
他扯了扯网的细绳
and at last the net rose to the top of the water
最后，网上升到水面
But there were no fish in his net
但他的网里没有鱼
nor was there a monster or thing of horror
也没有怪物或恐怖的东西
there was only a little Mermaid
只有一条小美人鱼
she was lying fast asleep in his net
她躺在他的网里睡着了
Her hair was like a wet foil of gold
她的头发像湿漉漉的金箔
like golden flakes in a glass of water
就像一杯水中的金色薄片
Her little body was as white ivory
她小小的身躯像白色的象牙
and her tail was made of silver and pearl
她的尾巴是用银和珍珠做的
and the green weeds of the sea coiled round her tail
海中的绿色杂草缠绕在她的尾巴上

and like sea-shells were her ears
她的耳朵就像贝壳一样
and her lips were like sea-coral
她的嘴唇像海珊瑚
The cold waves dashed over her cold breasts
寒潮拂过她冰冷的乳房
and the salt glistened upon her eyelids
盐在她的眼睑上闪闪发光
She was so beautiful that the he was filled with wonder
她是如此美丽，以至于他充满了惊奇
he pulled the net closer to the boat
他把网拉得更靠近船
leaning over the side, he clasped her in his arms
他侧身，将她紧紧抱在怀里
She woke, and looked at him in terror
她醒了过来，惊恐地看着他
When he touched her she gave a cry
当他碰到她时，她哭了起来
she cried out like a startled sea-gull
她像一只受惊的海鸥一样叫了起来
she looked at him with her mauve-amethyst eyes
她用紫水晶般的眼睛看着他
and she struggled so that she might escape
她挣扎着逃跑
But he held her tightly to him
但他紧紧地抱着她
and he did not allow her to depart
他不允许她离开
She wept when she saw she couldn't escape
当她看到自己无法逃脱时，她哭了
"I pray thee, let me go"
"我祈求你，放过我"
"I am the only daughter of a King"
"我是国王的独生女"
"please, my father is aged and alone"
"拜托，我父亲年纪大了，孤身一人"

- 3 -

But the young Fisherman would not let her go
但年轻的渔夫不肯放过她
"I will not let thee go unless you make me a promise"
"除非你答应我,否则我不会放过你"
"whenever I call thee thou wilt come and sing to me"
"每当我呼唤你时,你就要来为我歌唱"
"because your song delights the fishes"
"因为你的歌使鱼儿高兴"
"they come to listen to the song of the Sea-folk"
"他们来听海民的歌"
"and then my nets shall be full"
"然后我的网就满了"
the little mermaid saw that she had no choice
小美人鱼见她别无选择
"Would thou truly let me go if I promise this?"
"如果我答应了,你真的会放过我吗?"
"In very truth I will let thee go," he premised
"说实话,我会放过你,"他假设
So she made him the promise he desired
所以她给了他他想要的承诺
and she swore to do it by the oath of the Sea-folk
她发誓要按照海民的誓言去做
the young Fisherman loosened his arms from the mermaid
年轻的渔夫从美人鱼身上松开了手臂
the little mermaid sank back down into the water
小美人鱼又沉入水中
and she trembled with a strange kind of fear
她因一种奇怪的恐惧而颤抖

Every evening the young Fisherman went out upon the sea
每天傍晚,年轻的渔夫出海
and every evening he called out to the mermaid
每天晚上,他都呼唤美人鱼
the mermaid rose out of the water and sang to him
美人鱼从水里升起,给他唱歌
Round and round her swam the dolphins

海豚在她周围游来游去
and the wild gulls flew above her head
野生海鸥飞过她的头顶
she sang a marvellous song of the Sea-folk
她唱了一首美妙的海民歌
mermen who drive their flocks from cave to cave
将羊群从一个洞穴赶到另一个洞穴的人鱼
mermen who carry the little calves on their shoulders
肩上扛着小牛犊的人鱼
she sang of the Tritons who have long green beards
她唱着留着长长的绿色胡须的特里顿人
and she sang of the Triton's hairy chests
她唱着特里顿毛茸茸的胸膛
they blow through twisted conchs when the King passes
当国王经过时,它们会吹过扭曲的海螺
she sang of the palace of the King
她歌颂国王的宫殿
the palace which is made entirely of amber
宫殿完全由琥珀制成
the palace has a roof of clear emerald
宫殿有一个透明的翡翠屋顶
and it has a pavement of bright pearl
它有一条明亮的珍珠路面
and she sang of the gardens of the sea
她歌颂海边的花园
gardens where great fans of coral wave all day long
花园里,珊瑚的忠实粉丝整天都在挥手
and fish dart about like silver birds
鱼儿像银鸟一样飞来飞去
and the anemones cling to the rocks
海葵紧贴着岩石
She sang of the big whales that come from the north
她歌颂来自北方的大鲸鱼
they have sharp icicles hanging from their fins
它们的鳍上挂着锋利的冰柱
she sang of the Sirens who tell of wonderful things
她歌颂了讲述奇妙事物的海妖

so wonderful that merchants block their ears with wax
太棒了,商人用蜡堵住了耳朵
they block their ears so that they can not hear them
他们堵住耳朵,这样他们就听不到了
because if they heard them they would leap into the water
因为如果他们听到他们的声音,他们就会跳进水里
and they would be drowned in the sea
他们会被淹死在海里
she sang of the sunken galleys with their tall masts
她用高高的桅杆唱着沉没的厨房
she sang of the frozen sailors clinging to the rigging
她唱着冰冻的水手紧紧抓住索具
she sang the mackerel swimming through shipwrecks
她唱着鲭鱼在沉船中游来游去
she sang of the little barnacles travelling the world
她唱着环游世界的小藤壶
the barnacles cling to the keels of the ships
藤壶紧贴在船的龙骨上
and the ships go round and round the world
船只环游世界
and she sang of the cuttlefish in the sides of the cliffs
她唱着悬崖边上的墨鱼
and they stretch out their long black arms
他们伸出长长的黑色手臂
they can make night come when they will it
他们可以在他们愿意的时候让黑夜来临
She sang of the nautilus, who has a boat of her own
她歌颂鹦鹉螺号,鹦鹉螺号有自己的船
a boat that is carved out of an opal
用蛋白石雕刻而成的船
and the boat is steered with a silken sail
船是用丝帆操纵的
she sang of the happy Mermen who play upon harps
她歌颂了弹奏竖琴的快乐人鱼
they can charm the great Kraken to sleep
它们可以吸引大海妖入睡

she sang of the little children riding the porpoises
她唱着骑着海豚的小孩

the little children laugh as the ride the porpoises
小孩子们在骑海豚时笑着

she sang of the Mermaids who lie in the white foam
她歌颂躺在白色泡沫中的美人鱼

and they hold out their arms to the mariners
他们向水手们伸出双臂

she sang of the sea-lions with their curved tusks
她用弯曲的獠牙歌唱海狮

and she sang of the sea-horses with their floating manes
她歌颂着海马飘浮的鬃毛

When she sang the fishes came from the sea
当她唱歌时，鱼儿从海里来

the fish came to listen to her
鱼儿来听她说话

the young Fisherman threw his nets round them
年轻的渔夫把网扔在他们周围

and he caught as many fish as he needed
他尽可能多地捕到鱼

when his boat was full the Mermaid sunk back down
当他的船装满时，美人鱼又沉了下去

she went back down into the sea smiling at him
她回到海里，对他微笑

She never got close enough for him to touch her
她从来没有靠近到足以让他碰到她

Often times he called to the little mermaid
他经常呼唤小美人鱼

and he begged to her to come closer to him
他恳求她靠近他

but she dared not come closer to him
但她不敢靠近他

when he tried to catch her she dived into the water
当他试图抓住她时，她跳进了水里

just like when a seal dives into the sea

就像海豹潜入海中一样
and he wouldn't see her again that day
那天他再也见不到她了

each day her voice became sweeter to his ears
她的声音一天比一天甜美
Her voice so sweet that he forgot his nets
她的声音如此甜美，以至于他忘记了他的网
and he forgot his cunning and his craft
他忘记了自己的狡猾和手艺
The tuna went past him in large shoals
金枪鱼在大片的浅滩中从他身边经过
but he didn't pay any attention to them
但他没有理会他们
His spear lay by his side, unused
他的长矛躺在他身边，没有使用过
and his baskets of plaited osier were empty
他的篮子里有辫子的osier是空的
With lips parted, he sat idle in his boat
他张开嘴唇，无所事事地坐在船上
he listened to the songs of the mermaid
他听了美人鱼的歌
and his eyes were dim with wonder
他的眼睛因惊奇而昏暗
he listened till the sea-mists crept round him
他听着，直到海雾在他周围爬行
the wandering moon stained his brown limbs with silver
流浪的月亮将他棕色的四肢染成银色

One evening he called to the mermaid
一天晚上，他呼唤美人鱼
"Little Mermaid, I love thee," he professed
"小美人鱼，我爱你，"他自称
"Take me for thy bridegroom, for I love thee"
"娶我为新郎，因为我爱你"
But the mermaid shook her head

但美人鱼摇了摇头
"Thou hast a human Soul," she answered
"你有一个人类的灵魂,"她回答
"If only thou would send away thy Soul"
"要是你能送走你的灵魂就好了"
"if thy sent thy Soul away I could love thee"
"如果你把你的灵魂送走,我就可以爱你"
And the young Fisherman said to himself
年轻的渔夫对自己说
"of what use is my Soul to me?"
"我的灵魂对我有什么用?"
"I cannot see my Soul"
"我看不见我的灵魂"
"I cannot touch my Soul"
"我不能触碰我的灵魂"
"I do not know my Soul"
"我不认识我的灵魂"
"I will send my Soul away from me"
"我会把我的灵魂从我身边送走"
"and much gladness shall be mine"
"我必大喜乐"
And a cry of joy broke from his lips
一声喜悦的呼喊从他的嘴里爆发出来
he held out his arms to the Mermaid
他向美人鱼伸出双臂
"I will send my Soul away," he cried
"我会把我的灵魂送走,"他喊道
"you shall be my bride, and I will be thy bridegroom"
"你要做我的新娘,我要做你的新郎"
"in the depth of the sea we will dwell together"
"在大海的深处,我们将一起居住"
"all that thou hast sung of thou shalt show me"
"你所唱的一切,都要给我看"
"and all that thou desirest I will do for you"
"你所渴望的一切,我都会为你做"
"our lives will not be divided no longer"

"我们的生活将不再分裂"
the little Mermaid laughed, full of delight
小美人鱼笑了起来，满脸喜悦
and she hid her face in her hands
她把脸藏在手里
but the Fisherman didn't know how to send his Soul away
但渔夫不知道如何把他的灵魂送走
"how shall I send my Soul from me?"
"我该如何把我的灵魂从我身边送走呢？"
"Tell me how I can do it"
"告诉我我该怎么做"
"tell me how and it shall be done"
"告诉我怎么做，怎么做"
"Alas! I know not" said the little Mermaid
"唉！我不知道，"小美人鱼说
"the Sea-folk have no Souls"
"海民没有灵魂"
And she sank down into the sea
然后她沉入海里
and she looked up at him wistfully
她满怀憧憬地抬头看着他

The Priest
牧师

Early on the next morning
第二天一大早
before the sun was above the hills
在太阳升到山上之前
the young Fisherman went to the house of the Priest
年轻的渔夫去了牧师的家
he knocked three times at the Priest's door
他在牧师的门上敲了三下门
The Priest looked out through the door
牧师透过门向外望去
when he saw who it was he drew back the latch
当他看到是谁时，他拉回了门闩
and he welcomed the young Fisherman into his house
他欢迎年轻的渔夫到他家里来
he knelt down on the sweet-smelling rushes of the floor
他跪在地板上散发着甜美气味的冲动上
and he cried to the Priest, "Father"
他向祭司喊道："父啊"
"I am in love with one of the Sea-folk"
"我爱上了一个海民"
"and my Soul hindereth me from having my desire"
"我的灵魂阻碍我实现我的愿望"
"Tell me, how I can send my Soul away from me?"
"告诉我，我怎样才能把我的灵魂从我身边送走？"
"I truly have no need of it"
"我真的不需要它"
"of what use is my Soul to me?"
"我的灵魂对我有什么用？"
"I cannot see my Soul"
"我看不见我的灵魂"
"I cannot touch my Soul"
"我不能触碰我的灵魂"
"I do not know my Soul"

- 11 -

"我不认识我的灵魂"
And the Priest beat his chest
牧师捶胸顿足
and he answered, "thou art mad"
"他回答说:"你疯了""
"perhaps you have eaten poisonous herbs!"
"也许你吃了有毒的草药!"
"the Soul is the noblest part of man"
"灵魂是人最崇高的部分"
"and the Soul was given to us by God"
"灵魂是上帝赐给我们的"
"so that we nobly use our Soul"
"这样我们才能高尚地使用我们的灵魂"
"There is no thing more precious than a human Soul"
"没有什么比人类的灵魂更珍贵的了"
"It is worth all the gold that is in the world"
"世界上所有的黄金都值得"
"it is more precious than the rubies of the kings"
"它比国王的红宝石更珍贵"
"Think not any more of this matter, my son"
"不要再想这件事了,我的儿子"
"because it is a sin that may not be forgiven"
"因为这是一种不可饶恕的罪"
"And as for the Sea-folk, they are lost"
"至于海民,他们迷路了"
"and those who live with them are also lost"
"和他们住在一起的人也迷失了"
"They are like the beasts of the field"
"他们就像田野里的野兽"
"the beasts that don't know good from evil"
"不分善恶的野兽"
"the Lord has not died for their sake"
"耶和华没有为他们而死"

he heard the bitter words of the Priest
他听见了祭司的苦涩话语

the young Fisherman's eyes filled with tears
年轻的渔夫的眼睛里充满了泪水

he rose up from his knees and spoke, "Father"
他从膝盖上站起来,说:"父亲"

"the fauns live in the forest, and they are glad"
"牧神住在森林里,他们很高兴"

"on the rocks sit the Mermen with their harps of gold"
"岩石上坐着人鱼和他们的金竖琴"

"Let me be as they are, I beseech thee"
"让我像他们一样,我恳求你"

"their days are like the days of flowers"
"他们的日子就像鲜花的日子"

"And, as for my Soul," the young Fisherman continued
"至于我的灵魂,"年轻的渔夫继续说

what doth my Soul profit me?"
我的灵魂对我有什么好处呢?

"how is it good if it stands between what I love?"
"如果它挡在我所爱的东西之间,那又有什么好处呢?"

"The love of the body is vile" cried the Priest
"对身体的爱是卑鄙的,"神父喊道

"and vile and evil are the pagan things"
"卑鄙和邪恶是异教徒的事情"

"Accursed be the fauns of the woodland"
"林地里的牧神是被诅咒的"

"and accursed be the singers of the sea!"
"海中的歌唱者被诅咒了!"

"I have heard them at night-time"
"我在晚上听到了他们的声音"

"they have tried to lure me from my bible"
"他们试图引诱我从圣经中逃脱"

"They tap at the window, and laugh"
"他们敲了敲窗户,然后笑了"

"They whisper into my ears at night"
"他们晚上在我耳边低语"

"they tell me tales of their perilous joys"
"他们向我讲述了他们危险的快乐故事"

- 13 -

"They try to tempt me with temptations"
"他们试图用诱惑来诱惑我"

"and when I try to pray they mock me"
"当我试图祈祷时,他们嘲笑我"

"The mer-folk are lost, I tell thee"
"人鱼族迷路了,我告诉你"

"For them there is no heaven, nor hell"
"对他们来说,没有天堂,也没有地狱"

"and they shall never praise God's name"
"他们永远不赞美神的名"

"Father," cried the young Fisherman
"父亲,"年轻的渔夫喊道

"thou knowest not what thou sayest"
"你不知道你说什么"

"Once in my net I snared the daughter of a King"
"一旦我落入我的网中,我网罗了一位国王的女儿"

"She is fairer than the morning star"
"她比晨星还白皙"

"and she is whiter than the moon"
"她比月亮还白"

"For her body I would give my Soul"
"为了她的身体,我愿意献出我的灵魂"

"and for her love I would surrender heaven"
"为了她的爱,我愿意降服天堂"

"Tell me what I ask of thee"
"告诉我我对你的要求"

"Father I implore thee, let me go in peace"
"父亲,我恳求你,让我平安地走吧"

"Get away from me! Away!" cried the Priest
"离我远点!走开!"神父喊道

"thy lover is lost, and thou shalt be lost with her"
"你的爱人迷失了,你也要和她一起迷失"

the Priest gave him no blessing
祭司没有给他祝福

and he drove him from his door
他把他赶出了家门

the young Fisherman went down into the market-place
年轻的渔夫下到集市上去
he walked slowly with his head bowed
他低着头慢慢地走着
he walked like one who is in sorrow
他走路像一个忧愁的人
the merchants saw the young Fisherman coming
商人看到年轻的渔夫来了
and the merchants whispered to each other
商人们互相窃窃私语
one of the merchants came forth to meet him
一个商人出来迎接他
and he called him by his name
他直呼他的名字
"What hast thou to sell?" he asked him
"你要卖什么？"他问他
"I will sell thee my Soul," he answered
"我要把我的灵魂卖给你，"他回答
"I pray thee buy my Soul off me"
"我祈求你把我的灵魂从我身上买下来"
"because I am weary of it"
"因为我厌倦了"
"of what use is my Soul to me?"
"我的灵魂对我有什么用？"
"I cannot see my Soul"
"我看不见我的灵魂"
"I cannot touch my Soul"
"我不能触碰我的灵魂"
"I do not know my Soul"
"我不认识我的灵魂"
But the merchants only mocked him
但商人只是嘲笑他
"Of what use is a man's Soul to us?"
"人的灵魂对我们有什么用？"
"It is not worth a piece of silver"

"不值一块银子"

"Sell us thy body for slavery"
"把你的身体卖给我们做奴隶"

"and we will clothe thee in sea-purple"
"我们要给你穿上海紫色的衣服"

"and we'll put a ring upon thy finger"
"我们会在你的手指上戴上戒指"

"and we'll make thee the minion of the great Queen"
"我们会让你成为伟大女王的仆从"

"but don't talk of the Soul to us"
"但不要和我们谈论灵魂"

"because for us a Soul is of no use"
"因为对我们来说，灵魂是没有用的"

And the young Fisherman thought to himself
年轻的渔夫心想

"How strange a thing this is!"
"这真奇怪！"

"The Priest told me the value of the Soul"
"神父告诉我灵魂的价值"

"the Soul is worth all the gold in the world"
"灵魂值得世界上所有的黄金"

"but the merchants say a different thing"
"但商人说的是另一回事"

"the Soul is not worth a piece of silver"
"灵魂不值一分钱"

And he went out of the market-place
然后他走出了市场

and he went down to the shore of the sea
他下到海边

and he began to ponder on what he should do
他开始思考他应该怎么做

The Witch
女巫

At noon he remembered one of his friends
中午时分,他想起了他的一个朋友
his friend was a gatherer of samphire
他的朋友是海蓬子的采集者
he had told him of a young Witch
他告诉他一个年轻的女巫
this young Witch dwelt in a nearby cave
这个年轻的女巫住在附近的一个山洞里
and she was very cunning in her Witcheries
而且她在巫术中非常狡猾
the young Fisherman stood up and ran to the cave
年轻的渔夫站起身来,向山洞跑去

By the itching of her palm she knew he was coming
通过她手掌的痒痒,她知道他要来了
and she laughed, and let down her red hair
她笑了,放下了她的红发
She stood at the opening of the cave
她站在洞口处
her long red hair flowed around her
她的红色长发在她周围飘动
and in her hand she had a spray of wild hemlock
她手里拿着一朵野铁杉
"What do you lack?" she asked, as he came
"你缺什么?"当他走过来时,她问道
he was panting when got to her
当他走到她身边时,他气喘吁吁
and he bent down before her
他在她面前弯下腰
"Do you want fish for when there is no wind?"
"没有风的时候,你想钓鱼吗?"
"I have a little reed-pipe"
"我有一根小芦苇管"

"when I blow it the mullet come into the bay"
"当我吹它时，鲻鱼就会进入海湾"
"But it has a price, pretty boy"
"但它是有代价的，漂亮的男孩"
"What do you lack?"
"你缺什么？"

"Do you want a storm to wreck the ships?"
"你想让暴风雨毁坏船只吗？"
"It will wash the chests of rich treasure ashore"
"它会把富贵的宝箱冲上岸"
"I have more storms than the wind"
"我的风暴比风还多"
"I serve one who is stronger than the wind"
"我侍奉比风更强的人"
"I can send the great galleys to the bottom of the sea"
"我可以把大桨帆船送到海底"
"with a sieve and a pail of water"
"用筛子和一桶水"
"But I have a price, pretty boy"
"但是我是有代价的，漂亮的男孩"
"What do you lack?"
"你缺什么？"

"I know a flower that grows in the valley"
"我知道一朵花生长在山谷里"
"no one knows of this flower, but I"
"没有人知道这朵花，只有我"
"this secret flower has purple leaves"
"这朵秘花有紫色的叶子"
"and in the heart of the flower is a star"
"在花的心里有一颗星星"
"and its juice is as white as milk"
"它的汁液像牛奶一样白"
"touch the lips of the Queen with it"
"用它触摸女王的嘴唇"

"and she will follow thee all over the world"
"她要跟着你走遍天下"
"Out of the bed of the King she would rise"
"她会从国王的床上起来"
"and over the whole world she would follow thee"
"她要跟从整个世界"
"But it has a price, pretty boy"
"但它是有代价的,漂亮的男孩"
"What do you lack?"
"你缺什么?"

"I can pound a toad in a mortar"
"我可以在研钵里捣蟾蜍"
"and I can make broth of the toad"
"我可以给蟾蜍做肉汤"
"stir the broth with a dead man's hand"
"用死人的手搅拌肉汤"
"Sprinkle it on thine enemy while he sleeps"
"趁敌人睡觉的时候,把它洒在他身上"
"and he will turn into a black viper"
"他会变成一条黑毒蛇"
"and his own mother will slay him"
"他自己的母亲会杀了他"
"With a wheel I can draw the Moon from heaven"
"用轮子,我可以从天上画月亮"
"and in a crystal I can show thee Death"
"在水晶中,我可以向你展示死亡"
"What do you lack?"
"你缺什么?"
"Tell me thy desire and I will give it to you"
"告诉我你的愿望,我会给你"
"and thou shalt pay me a price, pretty boy"
"你要付我一个代价,漂亮的孩子"

"My desire is but for a little thing"
"我的愿望只是为了一件小事"

"yet the Priest was angry with me"
"可是神父却生我的气"
"and he chased me away in anger"
"他生气地把我赶走了"
"My wish is but for a little thing"
"我的愿望只是为了一件小事"
"yet the merchants have mocked me"
"可是商人却嘲笑我"
"and they denied me my wish"
"他们拒绝了我的愿望"
"Therefore have I come to thee"
"所以我到你这里来"
"I came although men call thee evil"
"我来了，虽然人们说你是邪恶的"
"but whatever thy price is I shall pay it"
"但无论你的代价是什么，我都要付"
"What would'st thou?" asked the Witch
"你会干什么？"女巫问
and she came near to the Fisherman
她走近了渔夫
"I wish to send my Soul away from me"
"我想把我的灵魂从我身边送走"
The Witch grew pale, and shuddered
女巫脸色苍白，浑身颤抖
and she hid her face in her blue mantle
她把脸藏在蓝色的斗篷里
"Pretty boy, that is a terrible thing to do"
"漂亮的男孩，这是一件可怕的事情"
He tossed his brown curls and laughed
他甩了甩棕色的卷发，笑了起来
"My Soul is nought to me" he answered
"我的灵魂对我来说是虚无缥缈的，"他回答说
"I cannot see my Soul"
"我看不见我的灵魂"
"I cannot touch my Soul"
"我不能触碰我的灵魂"

"I do not know my Soul"
"我不认识我的灵魂"

the young Witch saw an opportunity
年轻的女巫看到了机会

"What would thou give me if I tell thee?"
"如果我告诉你,你会给我什么?"

and she looked down at him with her beautiful eyes
她用她美丽的眼睛俯视着他

"I will give thee five pieces of gold" he said
"我会给你五块金子,"他说

"and I will give thee my nets for fishing"
"我要把我的网给你捕鱼"

"and I will give thee the house where I live"
"我要把我住的房子给你"

"and you can have my boat"
"你可以拥有我的船"

"I will give thee all that I possess"
"我要把我所拥有的一切给你"

"Tell me how to get rid of my Soul"
"告诉我如何摆脱我的灵魂"

She laughed mockingly at him
她嘲弄地嘲笑他

and she struck him with the spray of hemlock
她用铁杉的喷雾击中了他

"I can turn the autumn leaves into gold"
"我可以把秋天的树叶变成金子"

"and I can weave the pale moonbeams into silver"
"我可以把苍白的月光编织成银色"

"He whom I serve is richer than all kings"
"我所侍奉的,比一切君王都富有"

"thy price be neither gold nor silver," he confirmed
"你的价格既不是金也不是银,"他确认道

"What then shall I give thee if?"
"那我该给你什么呢?"

"The Witch stroked his hair with her thin white hand"
"女巫用她纤细白皙的手抚摸着他的头发"

- 21 -

"Thou must dance with me, pretty boy," she murmured
"你必须和我一起跳舞,漂亮的孩子,"她喃喃自语

and she smiled at him as she spoke
她说话时对他微笑

"Nothing but that?" cried the young Fisherman
"除了这个,别无他物?"年轻的渔夫喊道

and he wondered why she didn't ask for more
他想知道她为什么不要求更多

"Nothing but that" she answered
"仅此而已,"她回答

and she smiled at him again
她又对他笑了笑

"Then at sunset we shall dance together"
"然后,在日落时分,我们将一起跳舞"

"And after we have danced thou shalt tell me"
"我们跳完舞后,你要告诉我"

"The thing which I desire to know"
"我想知道的事情"

the young Witch shook her head
年轻的女巫摇了摇头

"When the moon is full" she muttered
"当月亮圆的时候,"她咕哝着

Then she peered all round, and listened
然后她环顾四周,听着

A blue bird rose screaming from its nest
一只蓝色的鸟儿从巢中尖叫着升起

and the blue bird circled over the dunes
那只蓝色的鸟在沙丘上盘旋

and three spotted birds rustled in the grass
三只斑点鸟在草地上沙沙作响

and the birds whistled to each other
鸟儿们互相吹口哨

There was no other sound except for the sound of a wave
除了波浪声,没有其他声音

the wave was crushing pebbles
海浪压碎了鹅卵石

So she reached out her hand
于是她伸出手
and she drew him near to her
她把他拉近她
and she put her dry lips close to his ear
她把干涸的嘴唇贴近他的耳朵
"Tonight thou must come to the top of the mountain"
"今晚你必须到山顶去"
"It is a Sabbath, and He will be there"
"今天是安息日，他会在那里"
The young Fisherman was startled by what she said
年轻的渔夫被她的话吓了一跳
she showed him her white teeth and laughed
她向他展示了她洁白的牙齿，笑了起来
"Who is He of whom thou speakest?"
"你说的是谁？"
"It matters not," she answered
"没关系，"她回答
"Go there tonight," she told him
"今晚去那里，"她告诉他
"wait for me under the branches of the hornbeam"
"在鹅耳枥的树枝下等我"
"If a black dog runs towards thee don't panic"
"如果一只黑狗向你跑来，不要惊慌"
"strike the dog with willow and it will go away"
"用柳树打狗，它就会消失"
"If an owl speaks to thee don't answer it"
"如果猫头鹰对你说话，不要回答它"
"When the moon is full I shall be with thee"
"月圆时，我要与你同在"
"and we will dance together on the grass"
"我们将一起在草地上跳舞"
the young Fisherman agreed to do as she said
年轻的渔夫同意按照她说的去做
"But do you swear to tell me how to send my Soul away?"
"但你发誓要告诉我如何把我的灵魂送走吗？"

She moved out into the sunlight
她走到阳光下
and the wind rippled through her red hair
风涟漪穿过她的红发
"By the hoofs of the goat I swear it"
"我用山羊的蹄子发誓"
"Thou art the best of the Witches" cried the young Fisherman
"你是女巫中最好的,"年轻的渔夫喊道
"and I will surely dance with thee tonight"
"今晚我一定会和你跳舞"
"I would have preferred it if you had asked for gold"
"如果你要金子,我会更喜欢它"
"But if this is thy price I shall pay it"
"但如果这是你的价钱,我就要付钱"
"because it is but a little thing"
"因为这只是一件小事"
He doffed his cap to her and bent his head low
他把帽子摘给她,低着头
and he ran back to town with joy in his heart
他心里欢喜地跑回城里
And the Witch watched him as he went
女巫在他走的时候看着他
when he had passed from her sight she entered her cave
当他从她的视线中消失时,她进入了她的洞穴
she took out a mirror from a box
她从盒子里拿出一面镜子
and she set up the mirror on a frame
她把镜子放在一个框架上
She burned vervain on lighted charcoal before the mirror
她在镜子前用点燃的木炭烧马鞭草
and she peered through the coils of the smoke
她透过烟雾的线圈凝视着
after a time she clenched her hands in anger
过了一会儿,她愤怒地握紧了双手
"He should have been mine," she muttered
"他应该是我的,"她咕哝着

"I am as beautiful as she is"
"我和她一样漂亮"

When the moon had risen he left his hut
当月亮升起时,他离开了他的小屋
the young Fisherman climbed up to the top of the mountain
年轻的渔夫爬上了山顶
and he stood under the branches of the hornbeam
他站在鹅耳枥的树枝下
The sea lay at his feet like a disc of polished metal
大海像一个抛光的金属圆盘一样躺在他的脚下
the shadows of the fishing boats moved in the little bay
渔船的影子在小海湾里移动
A great owl with yellow eyes called him
一只黄色眼睛的大猫头鹰叫他
it called him by his name
它用他的名字称呼他
but he made the owl no answer
但他让猫头鹰没有回答
A black dog ran towards him and snarled
一只黑狗向他跑来,咆哮着
but he did not panic when the dog came
但当狗来时,他并没有惊慌失措
he struck the dog with a rod of willow
他用一根柳树竿打了狗
and the dog went away, whining
狗走开了,呜呜叫着

At midnight the Witches came flying through the air
午夜时分,女巫们在空中飞来飞去
they were like bats flying in the air
他们就像在空中飞翔的蝙蝠
"Phew!" they cried, as they landed on the ground
"呸!"他们倒在地上时喊道
"there is someone here that we don't know!"
"这里有一个我们不认识的人!"

and they sniffed around for the stranger
他们四处嗅探陌生人

they chattered to each other and made signs
他们互相喋喋不休，做手势

Last of all came the young Witch
最后是年轻的女巫

her red hair was streaming in the wind
她的红发在风中飘扬

She wore a dress of gold tissue
她穿着一件金色纸巾连衣裙

and her dress was embroidered with peacocks' eyes
她的裙子上绣着孔雀的眼睛

a little cap of green velvet was on her head
她头上戴着一顶绿色天鹅绒的小帽子

"Who is he?" shrieked the Witches when they saw her
"他是谁？"女巫们看到她时尖叫起来

but she only laughed, and ran to the hornbeam
但她只是笑了笑，跑向鹅耳枥

and she took the Fisherman by the hand
她拉着渔夫的手

she led him out into the moonlight
她把他领到月光下

and in the moonlight they began to dance
在月光下，他们开始跳舞

Round and round they whirled in their dance
他们一圈又一圈地在舞蹈中旋转

she jumped higher and higher into the air
她跳得越来越高

he could see the scarlet heels of her shoes
他能看到她鞋子的猩红色高跟鞋

Then came the sound of the galloping of a horse
然后传来一匹马疾驰的声音

but there was no horse to be seen
但是没有马可看

and he felt afraid, but he did not know why
他感到害怕，但他不知道为什么

"Faster," cried the Witch to him
"快点，"女巫对他喊道
and she threw her arms around his neck
她搂着他的脖子
and her breath was hot upon his face
她的气息在他脸上滚烫
"Faster, faster!" she cried again
"快点，快点！"她又喊了一声
the earth seemed to spin beneath his feet
大地似乎在他脚下旋转
and his thoughts grew more and more troubled
他的思绪越来越烦恼
out of nowhere a great terror fell on him
不知从哪里冒出一股巨大的恐惧降临在他身上
he felt some evil thing was watching him
他感觉到有什么邪恶的东西在看着他
and at last he became aware of something
最后，他意识到了什么
under the shadow of a rock there was a figure
在岩石的阴影下，有一个人影
a figure that he had not been there before
一个他以前从未去过的身影
It was a man dressed in a black velvet suit
那是一个穿着黑色天鹅绒西装的男人
it was styled in the Spanish fashion
它以西班牙时尚风格设计
the strangers face was strangely pale
陌生人的脸色异常苍白
but his lips were like a proud red flower
但他的嘴唇却像一朵骄傲的红花
He seemed weary of what he was seeing
他似乎对他所看到的感到厌倦
he was leaning back toying in a listless manner
他无精打采地向后靠着玩弄
he was toying with the pommel of his dagger
他正在玩弄他的七首的鞍头

- 27 -

on the grass beside him lay a plumed hat
在他身旁的草地上，放着一顶羽毛帽
and there were a pair of riding gloves with gilt lace
还有一副镀金蕾丝的骑马手套
they were sewn with seed-pearls
它们是用种子珍珠缝制的
A short cloak lined with sables hung from his shoulder
他的肩膀上挂着一件衬有紫貂的短斗篷
and his delicate white hands were gemmed with rings
他精致白皙的手上镶嵌着戒指
Heavy eyelids drooped over his eyes
沉重的眼睑垂在眼睛上
The young Fisherman watched the stranger
年轻的渔夫看着这个陌生人
just like when one is snared in a spell
就像一个人被咒语困住一样
At last the Fisherman's and the stranger's eyes met
渔夫和陌生人的目光终于相遇了
wherever he danced the eyes seemed to be on him
无论他跳舞到哪里，眼睛似乎都注视着他
He heard the Witch laugh wildly
他听到女巫狂笑
and he caught her by the waist
他抓住了她的腰
and he whirled her madly round and round
他疯狂地把她转了一圈又一圈
Suddenly a dog barked in the woods
突然，一只狗在树林里吠叫
and all the dancers stopped dancing
所有的舞者都停止了跳舞
they knelt down and kissed the man's hands
他们跪下来亲吻男人的手
As they did so a little smile touched his proud lips
当他们这样做时，他骄傲的嘴唇上露出了一丝微笑
like when a bird's wing touches the water
就像鸟的翅膀碰到水面一样
and it makes the water laugh a little

它让水笑了一下
But there was disdain in his smile
但他的笑容中带着不屑
He kept looking at the young Fisherman
他一直看着年轻的渔夫
"Come! let us worship" whispered the Witch
"来吧!让我们崇拜吧,"女巫低声说
and she led him up to the man
她把他领到那人面前
a great desire to follow her seized him
追随她的强烈欲望抓住了他
and he followed her to the man
他跟着她去找那个男人
But when he came close he made the sign of the Cross
但当他走近时,他做了十字架的标志
he did this without knowing why he did it
他这样做时不知道他为什么要这样做
and he called upon the holy name
他呼求圣名
As soon as he did this the Witches screamed like hawks
他一这样做,女巫们就像鹰一样尖叫起来
and all the Witches flew away like bats
所有的女巫都像蝙蝠一样飞走了
the figure under the shadow tWitched with pain
阴影下的身影被痛苦地迷住了
The man went over to a little wood and whistled
那人走到一根小木头前,吹起了口哨
A horse with silver trappings came running to meet him
一匹披着银色衣服的马跑过来迎接他
As he leapt upon the saddle he turned round
当他跳上马鞍时,他转过身来
and he looked at the young Fisherman sadly
他悲伤地看着年轻的渔夫
the Witch with the red hair also tried to fly away
红头发的女巫也试图飞走
but the Fisherman caught her by her wrists
但渔夫抓住了她的手腕

and he kept hold of her tightly
他紧紧地抱着她
"Let me loose!" she cried, "Let me go!"
"放开我!"她喊道,"放开我!"
"thou hast named what should not be named"
"你给不该命名的命名"
"and thou hast shown the sign that may not be looked at"
"你显明了不可看的神迹"
"I will not let thee go till thou hast told me the secret"
"在你告诉我秘密之前,我不会放过你"
"What secret?" said the Witch
"什么秘密?"女巫说
and she wrestled with him like a wild cat
她像野猫一样与他搏斗
and she bit her foam-flecked lips
她咬了咬她满是泡沫的嘴唇
"You know the secret," replied the Fisherman
"你知道这个秘密,"渔夫回答说
Her grass-green eyes grew dim with tears
她草绿色的眼睛因泪水而变得黯淡
"Ask me anything but that!" she begged of the Fisherman
"除了这个,别问我什么!"她恳求渔夫
He laughed, and held her all the more tightly
他笑了,把她抱得更紧了
She saw that she could not free herself
她看到她无法释放自己
when she realized this she whispered to him
当她意识到这一点时,她低声对他说
"Surely I am as fair as the daughters of the sea"
"当然,我和海的女儿一样公平"
"and I am as comely as those that dwell in the blue waters"
"我和那些住在蓝色海水里的人一样可爱"
and she fawned on him and put her face close to his
她讨好他,把脸贴近他的脸
But he thrust her back and replied to her
但他把她推了回去,回答了她

"If thou don't keep your promise I will slay thee"
"如果你不遵守你的诺言，我就杀了你"
"I will slay thee for a false Witch"
"我会为一个假女巫杀了你"
She grew gas rey as a blossom of the Judas tree
她把 gas rey 长成犹大树的花朵
and a strange shudder past through her body
一种奇怪的颤抖从她的身体中掠过
"if that is how you want it to be," she muttered
"如果这就是你想要的样子，"她咕哝着
"It is thy Soul and not mine"
"这是你的灵魂，不是我的灵魂"
"Do with your Soul as thou wish"
"随心所欲地用你的灵魂去做"
And she took from her girdle a little knife
她从腰带上拿出一把小刀
the knife had a handle of green viper's skin
这把刀的刀柄是绿毒蛇的皮肤
and she gave him this green little knife
她把这把绿色的小刀给了他
"What shall I do with this?" he asked of her
"我该怎么办呢？"他问她
She was silent for a few moments
她沉默了一会儿
a look of terror came over her face
她的脸上露出惊恐的表情
Then she brushed her hair back from her forehead
然后她把头发从额头上往后梳
and, smiling strangely, she spoke to him
然后，她奇怪地笑了笑，对他说话
"men call it the shadow of the body"
"男人称它为身体的影子"
"but it is not the shadow of the body"
"但这不是身体的影子"
"the shadow is the body of the Soul"
"影子是灵魂的身体"

"Stand on the sea-shore with thy back to the moon"
"背对着月亮站在海边"

"cut away from around thy feet thy shadow"
"从你脚边剪下你的影子"

"the shadow, which is thy Soul's body"
"影子,是你灵魂的身体"

"and bid thy Soul to leave thee"
"吩咐你的灵魂离开你"

"and thy Soul will leave thee"
"你的灵魂会离开你"

The young Fisherman trembled, "Is this true?"
年轻的渔夫颤抖着说:"这是真的吗?

"what I have said is true," she answered him
"我说的是真的,"她回答他

"and I wish that I had not told thee of it"
"我希望我没有告诉你这件事"

she cried, and clung to his knees weeping
她哭了,紧紧抱着他的膝盖哭泣

he moved her away from him in the tall grass
他把她从高高的草丛中移开

and he placed the little green knife in his belt
他把那把绿色的小刀放在腰带上

then he went to the edge of the mountain
然后他走到山的边缘

from the edge of the mountain he began to climb down
他从山的边缘开始往下爬

The Soul
心灵

his Soul called out to him
他的灵魂呼唤着他
"I have dwelt with thee for all these years"
"这些年来,我一直与你同住"
"and I have been thy servant"
"我曾是你的仆人"
"Don't send me away from thee"
"不要让我离开你"
"what evil have I done thee?"
"我做了什么坏事?"
And the young Fisherman laughed
年轻的渔夫笑了
"Thou has done me no evil"
"你没有作恶我"
"but I have no need of thee"
"但我不需要你"
"The world is wide"
"世界很广阔"
"there is Heaven and Hell in this life"
"今生有天堂和地狱"
"and there a dim twilight between them"
"他们之间有一片昏暗的暮色"
"Go wherever thou wilt, but trouble me not"
"你想去哪里就去哪里,但不要麻烦我"
"because my love is calling to me"
"因为我的爱在呼唤我"
His Soul besought him piteously
他的灵魂可怜兮兮地恳求他
but the young Fishmerman heeded it not
但年轻的鱼人没有理会
instead, he leapt from crag to crag
相反,他从一个峭壁跳到另一个峭壁
he moved as sure-footed as a wild goat

他像野山羊一样稳重地走着
and at last he reached the level ground
最后，他到达了平地
and then he reached the yellow shore of the sea
然后他到达了黄色的海边
He stood on the sand with his back to the moon
他背对着月亮站在沙滩上
and out of the sea-foam came white arms
从海泡中走出了白色的手臂
the arms of the mermaid beckoned him to come
美人鱼的手臂招呼他过来
Before him lay his shadow; the body of his Soul
在他面前是他的影子;他灵魂的身体
behind him hung the moon, in honey-coloured air
在他身后挂着月亮，在蜂蜜色的空气中
And his Soul spoke to him again
他的灵魂再次对他说话
"thou hast decided to drive me away from thee"
"你决定把我从你身边赶走"
"but send me not forth without a heart"
"但不要无心地差遣我出去"
"The world you are sending me to is cruel"
"你送我去的世界是残酷的"
"give me thy heart to take with me"
"把你的心交给我带走"
He tossed his head and smiled
他摇了摇头，笑了笑
"With what should I love if I gave thee my heart?"
"如果我把我的心交给你，我应该爱什么？"
"Nay, but be merciful," said his Soul
"不，但要怜悯，"他的灵魂说
"give me thy heart, for the world is very cruel"
"把你的心给我，因为世界很残酷"
"and I am afraid," begged his soul
"我害怕，"他的灵魂乞求道
"My heart belongs my love," he answered

"我的心属于我的爱,"他回答
"Should I not love also?" asked his Soul
"我难道不应该也爱吗?"他的灵魂问道
but the fisherman didn't answer his soul
但渔夫没有回答他的灵魂
"Get thee gone, for I have no need of thee"
"把你带走,因为我不需要你"
and he took the little knife
他拿起了那把小刀
the knife with its handle of green viper's skin
这把刀柄是绿色的蝰蛇皮
and he cut away his shadow from around his feet
他从脚边剪掉了他的影子
and his shadow rose up and stood before him
他的影子升起,站在他面前
his shadow was just like he was
他的影子就像他一样
and his shadow looked just like he did
他的影子看起来就像他一样
He crept back and put his knife into his belt
他蹑手蹑脚地往后退,把刀腰带里
A feeling of awe came over him
一种敬畏的感觉笼罩着他
"Get thee gone," he murmured
"把你走开,"他喃喃自语
"let me see thy face no more"
"让我再也看不到你的脸"
"Nay, but we must meet again," said the Soul
"不,但我们必须再次见面,"灵魂说
His Soul's voice was low and like a flute
他的灵魂声音低沉,像笛子
its lips hardly moved while it spoke
它的嘴唇在说话时几乎没有动过
"How shall we meet?" asked the young Fisherman
"我们怎么见面呢?"年轻的渔夫问道
"Thou wilt not follow me into the depths of the sea?"

"你不愿意跟着我到海的深处去吗?"
"Once every year I will come to this place"
"每年我都会来这个地方一次"
"I will call to thee," said the Soul
"我会呼唤你,"灵魂说
"It may be that thou will have need of me"
"也许你需要我"
the young Fishermam did not see a reason
年轻的费舍尔曼没有看到理由
"What need could I have of thee?"
"我能有什么需要你呢?"
"but be it as thou wilt"
"但愿你所愿"
he plunged into the deep dark waters
他跳进了漆黑的深水中
and the Tritons blew their horns to welcome him
特里顿人吹响了号角欢迎他
the little Mermaid rose up to meet her lover
小美人鱼站起来迎接她的爱人
she put her arms around his neck
她搂着他的脖子
and she kissed him on the mouth
她吻了吻他的嘴
His Soul stood on the lonely beach
他的灵魂站在寂寞的海滩上
his Soul watched them sink into the sea
他的灵魂看着他们沉入大海
then his Soul went weeping away over the marshes
然后他的灵魂在沼泽地上哭泣

After the First Year
第一年后

it had been one year since had he cast his soul away
自从他抛弃自己的灵魂以来,已经一年了
the Soul came back to the shore of the sea
灵魂回到了海边
and the Soul called to the young Fisherman
灵魂呼唤年轻的渔夫
the young Fisherman rose back out of the sea
年轻的渔夫从海里复活了
he asked his soul, "Why dost thou call me?"
他问他的灵魂:"你为什么叫我?"
And the Soul answered, "Come nearer"
灵魂回答说:"靠近一点"
"come nearer, so that I may speak with thee"
"走近一点,好让我和你说话"
"I have seen marvellous things"
"我见过奇妙的事情"
So the young Fisherman came nearer to his soul
于是,年轻的渔夫更接近他的灵魂
and he couched in the shallow water
他躺在浅水里
and he leaned his head upon his hand
他把头靠在他的手上
and he listened to his Soul
他听从了他的灵魂
and his Soul spoke to him
他的灵魂对他说话

When I left thee I turned East
当我离开你时,我转向东方
From the East cometh everything that is wise
一切有智慧的东西都从东方来
For six days I journeyed eastwards
我向东走了六天

- 37 -

on the morning of the seventh day I came to a hill
第七天早上，我来到一座小山上
a hill that is in the country of the Tartars
鞑靼人国的一座小山
I sat down under the shade of a tamarisk tree
我在一棵柽柳树的树荫下坐了下来
in order to shelter myself from the sun
为了遮挡阳光
The land was dry and had burnt up from the heat
土地是干燥的，被高温烧毁了
The people went to and fro over the plain
人们在平原上来回走动
they were like flies crawling on polished copper
它们就像苍蝇在抛光的铜上爬行
When it was noon a cloud of red dust rose
中午时分，一团红色的尘埃升起
When the Tartars saw it they strung their bows
鞑靼人一看，就拉起了弓
and they leapt upon their little horses
他们跳上他们的小马
they galloped to meet the cloud of red dust
他们疾驰而去，迎向红尘云
The women fled to the wagons, screamin
妇女们尖叫着逃到马车上
they hid themselves behind the felt curtains
他们把自己藏在毡帘后面
At twilight the Tartars returned to their camp
黄昏时分，鞑靼人回到了他们的营地
but five of them did not return
但其中五个人没有回来
many of them had been wounded
他们中的许多人都受伤了
They harnessed their horses to the wagons
他们把马拴在马车上
and they drove away hastily
他们匆匆忙忙地开车走了
Three jackals came out of a cave and peered after them

- 38 -

三只豺狼从山洞里出来，跟在他们身后
the jackals sniffed the air with their nostrils
豺狼用鼻孔嗅着空气
and they trotted off in the opposite direction
他们向相反的方向小跑
When the moon rose I saw a camp-fire
当月亮升起时，我看到一堆篝火
and I went towards the fire in the distance
我走向远处的火堆
A company of merchants were seated round the fire
一队商人围坐在火堆旁
the merchants were sitting on their carpets
商人坐在地毯上
Their camels were tied up behind them
他们的骆驼被绑在他们身后
and their servants were pitching tents in the sand
他们的仆人正在沙地上搭帐篷
As I came near them the chief rose up
当我走近他们时，酋长站了起来
he drew his sword and asked me my intentions
他拔出剑，问我的意图
I answered that I was a Prince in my own land
我回答说，我是自己土地上的王子
I said I had escaped from the Tartars
我说我从鞑靼人那里逃出来了
they had sought to make me their slave
他们想让我成为他们的奴隶
The chief smiled and showed me five heads
酋长笑了笑，给我看了五个脑袋
the heads were fixed upon long reeds of bamboo
头固定在长长的竹芦苇上
Then he asked me who was the prophet of God
然后他问我谁是上帝的先知
I answered him that it was, "Mohammed"
我回答说是"穆罕默德"
He bowed and took me by the hand
他鞠了一躬，拉着我的手

and he let me sit by his side
他让我坐在他身边

A servant brought me some mare's milk in a wooden-dish
一个仆人用木盘给我端来了一些马奶

and he brought a piece of lamb's flesh
他拿来一块羊肉

At daybreak we started on our journey
黎明时分，我们开始了我们的旅程

I rode on a red-haired camel, by the side of the chief
我骑着一头红毛骆驼，在酋长身边

a runner ran before us, carrying a spear
一个跑步者拿着长矛跑在我们面前

The men of war were on both sides of us
战争的人在我们两边

and the mules followed with the merchandise
骡子跟着商品

There were forty camels in the caravan
商队里有四十头骆驼

and the mules were twice forty in number
骡子的数量是四十的两倍

We went from the land of Tartars to the land of Gryphons
我们从鞑靼人的土地来到了狮鹫的土地

The folk of the Gryphons curse the Moon
狮鹫的人们诅咒月亮

We saw the Gryphons on the white rocks
我们在白色的岩石上看到了狮鹫

they were guarding their gold treasure
他们守卫着他们的黄金宝藏

And we saw the scaled Dragons sleeping in their caves
我们看到鳞片龙睡在他们的洞穴里

As we passed over the mountains we held our breath
当我们越过群山时，我们屏住了呼吸

so that the snow would not fall on us
这样雪就不会落在我们身上

and each man tied a veil over his eyes
每个人都在眼睛上系了面纱

when we passed through the valleys of the Pygmies
当我们穿过俾格米人的山谷时

and the Pygmies shot their arrows at us
俾格米人向我们射箭

they shot from the hollows of the trees
他们从树洞里射出

at night we heard the wild men beat their drums
晚上，我们听到野人敲鼓

When we came to the Tower of Apes we offered fruits
当我们来到人猿塔时，我们提供了水果

and those inthe tower of the Apes did not harm us
那些在人猿塔里的人并没有伤害我们

When we came to the Tower of Serpents we offered milk
当我们来到蛇塔时，我们提供了牛奶

and those in the tower of the Serpents let us go past
那些在蛇塔里的人让我们过去

Three times in our journey we came to the banks of the Oxus
在我们的旅途中，我们三次来到奥克苏斯河岸边

We crossed the river Oxus on rafts of wood
我们乘坐木筏渡过奥克苏斯河

The river horses raged and tried to slay us
河马怒吼，试图杀死我们

When the camels saw them they trembled
当骆驼看到它们时，它们颤抖着

The kings of each city levied tolls on us
每个城市的国王都向我们征收通行费

but they would not allow us to enter their gates
但他们不让我们进入他们的大门

They threw bread over the walls to us
他们把面包扔到墙上给我们

and they gave us little maize-cakes baked in honey
他们给了我们用蜂蜜烤的小玉米饼

and cakes of fine flour filled with dates
和装满枣子的细面粉蛋糕

For every hundred baskets we gave them a bead of amber
每一百个篮子，我们都会给他们一颗琥珀珠

When villagers saw us coming they poisoned the wells
村民们看到我们来了，就把水井里毒死了
and the villagers fled to the hill-summits
村民们逃到山顶
on our journey we fought with the Magadae
在我们的旅程中，我们与Magadae战斗
They are born old, and grow younger every year
他们生来就老了，而且每年都变年轻
they die when they are little children
他们在小时候就死了
and on our journey we fought with the Laktroi
在我们的旅程中，我们与拉克罗伊人作战
they say that the Laktroi are the sons of tigers
他们说 Laktroi 是老虎的儿子
and they paint themselves yellow and black
他们把自己涂成黄色和黑色
And on our journey we fought with the Aurantes
在我们的旅程中，我们与奥兰特人作战
they bury their dead on the tops of trees
他们把死者埋在树梢上
the Sun, who is their god, slays their buried
太阳，谁是他们的神，杀死了他们被埋葬的人
so they live in dark caverns
所以他们住在黑暗的洞穴里
And on our journey we fought with the Krimnians
在我们的旅程中，我们与克里姆尼亚人作战
the folk of the Krimnians worship a crocodile
克里姆尼亚人的民间崇拜鳄鱼
they give the crocodile earrings of green glass
他们给鳄鱼耳环绿色玻璃
they feed the crocodile with butter and fresh fowls
他们用黄油和新鲜家禽喂鳄鱼
we fought with the Agazonbae, who are dog-faced
我们和狗脸的 Agazonbae 战斗
and we fought with the Sibans, who have horses' feet
我们与有马蹄的西班人作战

and they can run swifter than the fastest horses
它们可以比最快的马跑得更快

A third of our army died in battle
我军三分之一在战斗中阵亡
a third of our army died from want of food
我军三分之一死于缺粮
The rest of our army murmured against me
我们军队的其他成员对我嘀咕着
they said that I had brought them an evil fortune
他们说我给他们带来了厄运
I took an adder from beneath a stone
我从一块石头下面拿了一个加法器
and I let the adder bite my hand
我让加法器咬我的手
When they saw I did not sicken they grew afraid
当他们看到我没有生病时,他们开始害怕
In the fourth month we reached the city of Illel
第四个月,我们到达了伊勒尔市
It was night time when we reached the city
我们到达城市时已是晚上
we arrived at the grove outside the city walls
我们来到了城墙外的小树林
the air in the city was sultry
城里的空气很闷热
because the Moon was travelling in Scorpion
因为月亮在蝎子里旅行
We took the ripe pomegranates from the trees
我们从树上摘下了成熟的石榴
and we broke them, and drank their sweet juices
我们把它们打碎,喝它们甜汁
Then we laid down on our carpets
然后我们躺在地毯上
and we waited for the dawn to come
我们等待黎明的到来
At dawn we rose and knocked at the gate of the city

黎明时分，我们起床敲响了城门
the gate was wrought out of red bronze
大门是用红青铜锻造的
and the gate had carvings of sea-dragons
城门上有海龙的雕刻
The guards looked down from the battlements
守卫们从城垛上往下看
and they asked us what our intentions were
他们问我们的意图是什么
The interpreter of the caravan answered
大篷车的翻译回答
we said we had come from the land of Syria
我们说我们来自叙利亚的土地
and we told him we had many merchandise
我们告诉他我们有很多商品
They took some of us as hostages
他们把我们中的一些人当作人质
and they told us they would open the gate at noon
他们告诉我们他们会在中午打开大门
when it was noon they opened the gate
到了中午，他们打开了大门
when we entered the people came out of the houses
当我们进去时，人们从房子里出来
they came in order to look at us
他们来是为了看我们
and a town crier went around the city
一个镇上的哭泣者在城里转了一圈
he made announcements of our arrival through a shell
他通过一个炮弹宣布了我们的到来
We stood in the market-place of the medina
我们站在麦地那的集市上
and the servants uncorded the bales of cloths
仆人解开了一捆捆布
they opened the carved chests of sycamore
他们打开了梧桐雕刻的箱子
Then merchants set forth their strange wares

然后，商人摆出他们奇怪的商品
waxed linen from Egypt, painted linen from the Ethiops
来自埃及的打蜡亚麻布，来自埃塞俄比亚的彩绘亚麻布
purple sponges from Tyre, cups of cold amber
来自提尔的紫色海绵，冷琥珀杯
fine vessels of glass, and curious vessels of burnt clay
精美的玻璃器皿和奇特的烧焦粘土器皿
From the roof of a house a company of women watched us
一群妇女从房子的屋顶上看着我们
One of them wore a mask of gilded leather
其中一人戴着镀金皮革面具

on the first day the Priests came and bartered with us
第一天，祭司们来了，和我们交换
On the second day the nobles came and bartered with us
第二天，贵族们来了，和我们以物易物
on the third day the craftsmen came and bartered with us
第三天，工匠们来了，和我们交换
all of them brought their slaves to us
他们都把他们的奴隶带到了我们这里
this is their custom with all merchants
这是他们对所有商家的习俗
we waited for the moon to come
我们等待月亮的到来
when the moon was waning I wandered away
当月亮渐渐消失时，我徘徊了
I wondered through the streets of the city
我在城市的街道上纳闷
and I came to the garden of the city's God
我来到了城神的花园
The Priests in their yellow robes moved silently
身穿黄色长袍的祭司们默默地移动着
they moved through the green trees
他们穿过绿树
There was a pavement of black marble
有一条黑色大理石的路面
and on this pavement stood a rose-red house

- 45 -

在这条人行道上矗立着一座玫瑰红色的房子
this was the house in which the God was dwelling
这是神所居住的房子
its doors were of powdered lacquer
它的门是粉漆的
and bulls and peacocks were wrought on the doors
公牛和孔雀被锻造在门上
and the doors were polished with gold
门是用金子打磨的
The tiled roof was of sea-green porcelain
瓦屋顶是海绿色的瓷器
and the jutting eaves were festooned with little bells
突出的屋檐上挂着小铃铛
When the white doves flew past they struck the bells
当白鸽飞过时，它们敲响了铃铛
they struck the bells with their wings
他们用翅膀敲打铃铛
and the doves made the bells tinkle
鸽子让铃铛叮叮当当
In front of the temple was a pool of clear water
寺庙前面是一潭清澈的水
the pool was paved with veined onyx
游泳池铺有脉络缟玛瑙
I laid down beside the water of the pool
我躺在水池边
and with my pale fingers I touched the broad leaves
我用苍白的手指摸了摸宽阔的叶子
One of the Priests came towards me
其中一位神父向我走来
and the priest stood behind me
牧师站在我身后
He had sandals on his feet
他脚上穿着凉鞋
one sandal was of soft serpent-skin
一双凉鞋是柔软的蛇皮
and the other sandal was of birds' plumage
另一只凉鞋是鸟的羽毛

On his head was a mitre of black felt
他的头上戴着一毡黑毡
and it was decorated with silver crescents
它装饰着银色的新月
Seven kinds of yellow were woven into his robe
他的长袍上编织了七种黄色
and his frizzed hair was stained with antimony
他卷曲的头发上沾满了锑

After a little while he spoke to me
过了一会儿，他对我说了一句话
finally, he asked me my desire
最后，他问我的愿望
I told him that my desire was to see their god
我告诉他，我的愿望是见到他们的神
He looked strangely at me with his small eyes
他用他的小眼睛奇怪地看着我
"The god is hunting," said the Priest
"神在打猎，"牧师说
I did not accept the answer of the priest
我没有接受神父的回答
"Tell me in what forest and I will ride with him"
"告诉我在哪个森林里，我会和他一起骑车"
his finger nails were long and pointed
他的指甲又长又尖
he combed out the soft fringes of his tunic
他梳理了上衣柔软的流苏
"The god is asleep," he murmured
"神睡着了，"他喃喃自语
"Tell me on what couch, and I will watch over him"
"告诉我在什么沙发上，我会看管他"
"The god is at the feast" he cried
"神在筵席上，"他喊道
"If the wine be sweet, I will drink it with him"
"如果酒是甜的，我会和他一起喝"
"and if the wine be bitter, I will drink it with him also"

"如果酒是苦的,我也要和他一起喝"
He bowed his head in wonder
他惊奇地低下了头
then he took me by the hand
然后他拉着我的手
and raised me up onto my feet
把我扶起来
and he led me into the temple
他领着我进了圣殿

In the first chamber I saw an idol
在第一个房间里,我看到了一个偶像
This idol was seated on a throne of jasper
这个偶像坐在碧玉的宝座上
the idol was bordered with great orient pearls
神像镶嵌着巨大的东方珍珠
and on its forehead was a great ruby
它的额头上有一颗巨大的红宝石
the idol was of a man, carved out of ebony
神像是一个男人,用乌木雕刻而成
thick oil dripped from its hair to its thighs
浓稠的油脂从头发滴到大腿
Its feet were red with the blood of a newly-slain lamb
它的脚被一只新杀的羔羊的血染红了
and its loins girt with a copper belt
它的腰部有一条铜带
copper that was studded with seven beryls
镶嵌着七个绿柱石的铜
And I said to the Priest, "Is this the god?"
我对神父说:"这是神吗?
And he answered me, "This is the god"
他回答我说:"这是神"
"Show me the god," I cried, "or I will slay thee"
"给我看看神,"我喊道,"否则我就杀了你。
I touched his hand and it withered
我摸了摸他的手,它就枯萎了
"Let my lord heal his servant," he begged me

"让我的主人医治他的仆人,"他恳求我
"heal his servant and I will show him the God"
"医治他的仆人,我就向他显明神"
So I breathed with my breath upon his hand
于是我用我的呼吸在他的手上呼吸
when I did this his hand became whole again
当我这样做时,他的手又变得完整了
and the priest trembled with fear
祭司吓得浑身发抖
Then he led me into the second chamber
然后他把我领进了第二个房间
in this chamber I saw another idol
在这个房间里,我看到了另一个偶像
The idol was standing on a lotus of jade
神像站在一朵莲花玉上
the lotus hung with great emeralds
莲花挂着巨大的祖母绿
and the lotus was carved out of ivory
莲花是用象牙雕刻而成的
its stature was twice the stature of a man
它的身材是男人的两倍
On its forehead was a great chrysolite
它的额头上有一块巨大的绿晶石
its breasts were smeared with myrrh and cinnamon
它的乳房上涂满了没药和肉桂
In one hand it held a crooked sceptre of jade
它一只手拿着一根弯曲的玉权杖
and in the other hand it held a round crystal
另一只手拿着一个圆形的水晶
and its thick neck was circled with selenites
它粗壮的脖子上环绕着亚硒酸盐
I asked the Priest, "Is this the god?"
我问神父:"这是神吗?
he answered me, "This is the god"
他回答我说:"这是神"
"Show me the god," I cried, "or I will slay thee"

"给我看看神，"我喊道，"否则我就杀了你。
And I touched his eyes and they became blind
我摸了摸他的眼睛，眼睛就瞎了
And the Priest begged me for mercy
神父恳求我怜悯
"Let my lord heal his servant"
"让我的主人医治他的仆人"
"heal me and I will show him the God"
"医治我，我要向他显明上帝"
So I breathed with my breath upon his eyes
于是我用呼吸呼吸着他的眼睛
and the sight came back to his eyes
眼前的景象又回到了他的眼前
He trembled with fear again
他又因恐惧而颤抖
and then he led me into the third chamber
然后他把我领进了第三个房间

There was no idol in the third chamber
第三个房间里没有偶像
there were no images of any kind
没有任何类型的图像
all there was in the room was a mirror
房间里只有一面镜子
the mirror was made of round metal
镜子由圆形金属制成
the mirror was set on an altar of stone
镜子被放在一个石头祭坛上
I said to the Priest, "Where is the god?"
我对神父说："神在哪里？"
he answered me, "There is no god but this mirror
他回答我说："除了这面镜子，没有神
because this is the Mirror of Wisdom
因为这是智慧的镜子
It reflects all things that are in heaven
它反映了天上的一切

and it reflects all things that are on earth
它反映了地球上的所有事物

except for the face of him who looketh into it
除了看着它的人的脸

him who looketh into it it reflects not
谁看它，它反映不

so he who looketh into the mirror will become wise
所以照镜子的人会变得聪明

there are many other mirrors in the world
世界上还有许多其他镜子

but they are mirrors of opinion
但它们是意见的镜子

This is the only mirror that shows Wisdom
这是唯一一面显示智慧的镜子

those who possess this mirror know everything
拥有这面镜子的人什么都知道

There isn't anything that is hidden from them
对他们来说没有什么是隐瞒的

And those who don't possess the mirror don't have Wisdom
而那些没有镜子的人就没有智慧

Therefore this mirror is the God
因此，这面镜子就是上帝

and that is why we worship this mirror
这就是我们崇拜这面镜子的原因

And I looked into the mirror
我照了照镜子

and it was as he had said to me
正如他对我说的那样

And then I did a strange thing
然后我做了一件奇怪的事情

but what I did matters not
但我做了什么并不重要

There a valley that is but a day's journey from here
那里有一个山谷，距离这里只有一天的路程

in this valley I have hidden the Mirror of Wisdom
在这个山谷里，我隐藏了智慧之镜

Allow me to enter into thee again
请允许我再次进入你

accept me and thou shalt be wiser than all the wise men
接受我,你就会比所有的智者都聪明

let me enter into thee and none will be as wise as thou
让我进入你里面,没有人会像你一样聪明

But the young Fisherman laughed
但年轻的渔夫笑了

"Love is better than Wisdom"
"爱胜于智慧"

"The little Mermaid loves me"
《小美人鱼爱我》

"But there is nothing better than Wisdom" said the Soul
"但没有什么比智慧更好的了,"灵魂说

"Love is better," answered the young Fisherman
"爱更好,"年轻的渔夫回答

and he plunged into the deep sea
他跳进了深海

and the Soul went weeping away over the marshes
灵魂在沼泽地上哭泣

After the Second Year
第二年后

it had been two years since he had cast his soul away
他已经两年没有抛弃自己的灵魂了
the Soul came back to the shore of the sea
灵魂回到了海边
and the Soul called to the young Fisherman
灵魂呼唤年轻的渔夫
the young Fisherman rose back out of the sea
年轻的渔夫从海里复活了
he asked his soul, "Why dost thou call me?"
他问他的灵魂:"你为什么叫我?
And the Soul answered, "Come nearer"
灵魂回答说:"靠近一点"
"come nearer, so that I may speak with thee"
"走近一点,好让我和你说话"
"I have seen marvellous things"
"我见过奇妙的事情"
So the young Fisherman came nearer to his soul
于是,年轻的渔夫更接近他的灵魂
and he couched in the shallow water
他躺在浅水里
and he leaned his head upon his hand
他把头靠在他的手上
and he listened to his Soul
他听从了他的灵魂
and his Soul spoke to him
他的灵魂对他说话

When I left thee I turned my face to the South
当我离开你时,我把脸转向南方
From the South cometh everything that is precious
一切珍贵的东西都来自南方
Six days I journeyed along the dusty paths
六天来,我沿着尘土飞扬的小路旅行

and the paths led to the city of Ashter
这些小路通向阿什特市

ways by which the pilgrims are wont to go
朝圣者不会去的方式

on the morning of the seventh day I lifted up my eyes
第七天早上，我抬起了眼睛

and lo! the city of Ashter lay at my feet
瞧！阿什特城就在我的脚下

because the city of Ashter is in a valley
因为阿什特市位于山谷中

There are nine gates around this city
这个城市周围有九个城门

in front of each gate stands a bronze horse
每扇门前都站着一匹青铜马

the horses neigh when the Bedouins come from the mountains
当贝都因人从山上来时，马匹会发出嘶嘶声

The walls of the city are cased with copper
城墙用铜包裹

the watch-towers on the walls are roofed with brass
墙上的瞭望塔是用黄铜盖的

In every tower along the wall stands an archer
在城墙上的每一座塔楼上都站着一个弓箭手

and each archer has a bow in his hand
每个弓箭手手里都拿着一把弓

At sunrise he strikes a gong with an arrow
日出时，他用箭敲锣

and at sunset he blows through a horn
日落时分，他吹响喇叭

when I sought to enter the guards stopped me
当我试图进入时，警卫拦住了我

and the guards asked of me who I was
警卫问我是谁

I made answer that I was a Dervish
我回答说我是苦行僧

I said I was on my way to the city of Mecca
我说我正在去麦加城的路上

in Mecca there was a green veil
在麦加,有一层绿色的面纱
the Koran was embroidered with silver letters on it
《古兰经》上绣着银色字母
it was embroidered by the hands of the angels
它是由天使的手绣制的
the guards were filled with wonder at what I told them
警卫们对我告诉他们的话充满了惊奇
and they entreated me to enter the city
他们恳求我进城
Inside the city there was a bazaar
城内有一个集市
Surely thou should'st have been with me
你当然应该和我在一起
in the narrow streets the happy paper lanterns flutter
狭窄的街道上,快乐的纸灯笼飘扬
they flutter like large butterflies
它们像大蝴蝶一样飞舞
When the wind blows they rise and fall like bubbles
当风吹来时,它们像泡泡一样起起落落
In front of their booths sit the merchants
在他们的摊位前坐着商人
every merchant sits on their silken carpets
每个商人都坐在他们的丝绸地毯上
They have long straight black beards
他们有长而直的黑胡须
and their turbans are covered with golden sequins
他们的头巾上覆盖着金色的亮片
they hold strings of amber and carved peach-stones
他们拿着一串琥珀和雕刻的桃子
and they glide them through their cool fingers
他们用冰凉的手指滑动它们
Some of them sell galbanum and nard
他们中的一些人出售galbanum和nard
some sell perfumes from the islands of the Indian Sea
有些出售来自印度海岛屿的香水

and they sell the thick oil of red roses and myrrh
他们出售浓稠的红玫瑰和没药油
and they sell little nail-shaped cloves
他们卖指甲形的小丁香
When one stops to speak to them they light frankincense
当一个人停下来和他们说话时，他们会点燃乳香
they throw pinches of it upon a charcoal brazier
他们把它捏在木炭火盆上
and it makes the air sweet
它使空气变得甜美
I saw a Syrian who held a thin rod
我看到一个拿着细棒的叙利亚人
grey threads of smoke came from the rod
灰色的烟雾从杆上冒出来
and its odour was like the odour of the pink almonds
它的气味就像粉红色杏仁的气味
Others sell silver bracelets embossed with turquoise stones
其他人则出售压印有绿松石的银手镯
and anklets of brass wire fringed with little pearls
和黄铜丝脚链，上面镶有小珍珠
and tigers' claws set in gold
和镶金的老虎爪子
and the claws of that gilt cat
还有那只镀金猫的爪子
the the claws of leopards, also set in gold
豹爪，同样镶嵌在黄金中
and earrings of pierced emerald
和穿孔祖母绿耳环
and finger-rings of hollowed jade
和镂空玉的指环
From the tea-houses came the sound of the guitar
从茶馆里传来了吉他的声音
and the opium-smokers were in the tea-houses
吸鸦片的人在茶馆里
their white smiling faces look out at the passers-by
他们洁白的笑脸望着路人

thou truly should'st have been with me
你真的应该和我在一起
The wine-sellers elbow their way through the crowd
卖酒的人在人群中蹒跚前行
with great black skins on their shoulders
肩膀上有黑色的皮肤
Most of them sell the wine of Schiraz
他们中的大多数出售Schiraz的葡萄酒
the wine of Schiraz is as sweet as honey
Schiraz的葡萄酒像蜂蜜一样甜
They serve it in little metal cups
他们把它放在小金属杯里
In the market-place stand the fruit sellers
在市场上，卖水果的人
the fruit sellers sell all kinds of fruit
卖水果的人卖各种水果
ripe figs, with their bruised purple flesh
成熟的无花果，果肉瘀伤的紫色
melons, smelling of musk and yellow as topazes
甜瓜，闻起来有麝香的味道，黄色像黄玉
citrons and rose-apples and clusters of white grapes
香橼、玫瑰苹果和一串串白葡萄
round red-gold oranges and oval lemons of green gold
圆形的红金橙子和椭圆形的柠檬绿金
Once I saw an elephant go by the fruit sellers
有一次，我看到一头大象从卖水果的人身边经过
Its trunk was painted with vermilion and turmeric
它的树干涂有朱砂和姜黄
and over its ears it had a net of crimson silk cord
它的耳朵上挂着一张深红色的丝线网
It stopped opposite one of the booths
它停在其中一个摊位对面
and the elephant began eating the oranges
大象开始吃橘子
instead of getting angry, the man only laughed
男人没有生气，只是笑了
Thou canst not think how strange a people they are

- 57 -

你不能想象他们是一个多么奇怪的民族
When they are glad they go to the bird-sellers
当他们高兴时,他们就会去找卖鸟的人
they go to them to buy a caged bird
他们去找他们买一只笼子里的鸟
and they set the bird free to increase their joy
他们放飞了鸟儿,以增加他们的喜乐
and when they are sad they scourge themselves with thorns
当他们悲伤时,他们用荆棘鞭打自己
so that their sorrow may not grow less
这样他们的忧愁就不会减少

One evening I met some slaves
一天晚上,我遇到了一些奴隶
they were carrying a heavy palanquin through the bazaar
他们抬着一顶沉重的轿子穿过集市
It was made of gilded bamboo
它是由镀金的竹子制成的
and the poles were of vermilion lacquer
杆子是朱红色的漆
it was studded with brass peacocks
它镶嵌着黄铜孔雀
Across the windows hung thin curtains
窗户上挂着薄薄的窗帘
the curtains were embroidered with beetles' wings
窗帘上绣着甲虫的翅膀
and they were lined with tiny seed-pearls
它们衬着细小的种子珍珠
and as it passed by a pale-faced Circassian smiled at me
当它经过时,一个脸色苍白的切尔克斯人对我微笑
I followed behind bearers of the palanquin
我跟在轿子的后面
and the slaves hurried their steps and scowled
奴隶们匆匆忙忙地走了脚步,皱起了眉头
But I did not care if they scowled
但我不在乎他们是否皱眉

I felt a great curiosity come over me
我感到一股强烈的好奇心涌上心头

At last they stopped at a square white house
最后，他们在一座方形的白色房子前停了下来

There were no windows to the house
房子没有窗户

all the house had was a little door
房子里只有一扇小门

and the door was like the door of a tomb
那扇门就像坟墓的门

They set down the palanquin at the house
他们在房子里放下了轿子

and they knocked three times with a copper hammer
他们用铜锤敲了三下

An Armenian in a green leather caftan peered through the wicket
一名身穿绿色皮革长衫的亚美尼亚人透过检票口窥视着

and when he saw them he opened the door
当他看到他们时，他打开了门

he spread a carpet on the ground and the woman stepped out
他在地上铺了一块地毯，那个女人走了出来

As she went in she turned round and smiled at me again
当她进去时，她转过身来，再次对我微笑

I had never seen anyone so pale
我从未见过如此苍白的人

When the moon rose I returned to the same place
当月亮升起时，我回到了同一个地方

and I sought for the house, but it was no longer there
我寻找那所房子，但它已经不在那里了

When I saw that I knew who the woman was
当我看到我知道那个女人是谁时

and I knew why she had smiled at me
我知道她为什么对我微笑

Certainly, thou should'st have been with me
当然，你应该和我在一起

There was a feast of the New Moon
有一场新月的盛宴
the young Emperor came forth from his palace
年轻的皇帝从他的宫殿里出来
and he went into the mosque to pray
他走进清真寺祈祷
His hair and beard were dyed with rose-leaves
他的头发和胡须都染上了玫瑰叶
and his cheeks were powdered with a fine gold dust
他的脸颊上沾满了细小的金粉
The palms of his feet and hands were yellow with saffron
他的脚掌和手掌是黄色的，上面有藏红花
At sunrise he went forth from his palace
日出时分，他从宫殿里出来
he was dressed in a robe of silver
他穿着一件银色的长袍
and at sunset he returned again
日落时分，他又回来了
then he was dressed in a robe of gold
然后他穿着一件金色的长袍
The people flung themselves on the ground
人们扑倒在地上
they hid their faces, but I would not do so
他们把脸藏起来，但我不会这样做
I stood by the stall of a seller of dates and waited
我站在一个卖枣子的摊位旁等着
When the Emperor saw me he raised his painted eyebrows
皇帝一见到我，就扬起了眉毛
and he stopped to observe me
他停下来观察我
I stood quite still and made him no obeisance
我站着不动，没有向他行礼
The people marvelled at my boldness
人们惊叹于我的胆量
they counselled me to flee from the city
他们劝我逃离城市

but I paid no heed to their warnings
但我没有理会他们的警告

instead, I went and sat with the sellers of strange gods
相反,我去和奇怪的神的卖家坐在一起

by reason of their craft they are abominated
由于他们的手艺,他们被憎恶

When I told them what I had done each of them gave me an idol
当我告诉他们我做了什么时,他们每个人都给了我一个偶像

and they prayed me to leave them
他们祈求我离开他们

That night I was in the Street of Pomegranates
那天晚上,我在石榴街

I was in a tea-house and I laid on a cushion
我在茶馆里,躺在垫子上

the guards of the Emperor entered and led me to the palace
皇帝的侍卫进来,把我带到了皇宫

As I went in they closed each door behind me
当我进去时,他们关上了我身后的每一扇门

and they put a chain across each door
他们在每扇门上都放了一条链子

Inside the palace there was a great courtyard
宫殿内有一个大院子

The walls of the courtyard were of white alabaster
院子的墙壁是白色的雪花石膏

the alabaster was decorated with blue and green tiles
雪花石膏装饰着蓝色和绿色的瓷砖

and the pillars were of green marble
柱子是绿色大理石的

and the pavement was of peach-blossom marble
路面是桃花大理石

I had never seen anything like it before
我以前从未见过这样的事情

As I passed the courtyard two veiled women were on a balcony
当我经过院子时,两个蒙着面纱的女人在阳台上

they looked down from their balcony and cursed me
他们从阳台上往下看,咒骂我
The guards hastened on through the courtyard
守卫们赶紧穿过院子
the butts of the lances rang upon the polished floor
长矛的枪托在抛光的地板上响起
They opened a gate of wrought ivory
他们打开了一扇锻造象牙的大门
I found myself in a watered garden of seven terraces
我发现自己置身于一个由七个梯田组成的浇水花园中
The garden was planted with tulip-cups and moon-flowers
花园里种满了郁金香杯和月亮花
a fountain hung in the dusky air like a slim reed of crystal
喷泉悬挂在昏暗的空气中,就像一根纤细的水晶芦苇
The cypress-trees were like burnt-out torches
柏树就像烧焦的火炬
From one of the trees a nightingale was singing
一只夜莺在一棵树上唱歌
At the end of the garden stood a little pavilion
花园的尽头矗立着一个小亭子
while we approached the pavilion two eunuchs came out
当我们走近亭子时,两个太监出来了
Their fat bodies swayed as they walked
他们肥胖的身体在走路时摇晃
and they glanced curiously at me
他们好奇地瞥了我一眼
One of them drew aside the captain of the guard
其中一人把警卫队长拉到一边
and in a low voice the eunuch whispered to him
太监低声对他低声说
The other kept munching scented pastilles
另一个人不停地咀嚼着有香味的锭剂
these he took out of an oval box of lilac enamel
这些他从椭圆形的淡紫色珐琅盒中取出
soon after the captain of the guard dismissed the soldiers
不久之后,卫队长解雇了士兵
The soldiers went back to the palace

士兵们回到了宫殿
the eunuchs followed behind the guards, but slowly
太监跟在侍卫身后,但速度很慢
and they plucked the sweet mulberries from the trees
他们从树上摘下甜桑葚
at one time the older eunuch turned round
有一次,年长的太监转过身来
and he smiled at me with an evil smile
他用邪恶的笑容对我笑了笑
Then the captain of the guards motioned me forwards
然后卫兵队长示意我往前走
I walked to the entrance without trembling
我颤抖地走到入口处
I drew the heavy curtain aside, and entered
我把厚重的窗帘拉到一边,走了进去
The young Emperor was stretched on a couch
年轻的皇帝在沙发上伸了个懒腰
the couch was covered in dyed lion skins
沙发上覆盖着染色的狮子皮
and a falcon was perched upon his wrist
一只猎鹰栖息在他的手腕上
Behind him stood a brass-turbaned Nubian
在他身后站着一个戴着黄铜头巾的努比亚人
he was naked down to the waist
他赤身裸体到腰部
he had heavy earrings in his split ears
他裂开的耳朵里戴着沉重的耳环
On a table by the side lay a mighty scimitar of steel
在旁边的桌子上放着一把强大的钢制弯刀
When the Emperor saw me he frowned
当皇帝看到我时,他皱起了眉头
he asked me, "What is thy name?"
他问我:"你叫什么名字?
"Knowest thou not that I am Emperor of this city?"
"你不知道我是这座城市的皇帝吗?"
But I made him no answer to his question

但我没有让他回答他的问题
He pointed with his finger at the scimitar
他用手指着弯刀
the Nubian seized the scimitar, ready to fight
努比亚人抓住了弯刀，准备战斗
rushing forward he struck at me with great violence
他冲上前去，用极大的暴力击打我
The blade whizzed through me and did me no hurt
刀刃在我身上呼啸而过，没有伤害到我
The man fell sprawling on the floor
这名男子瘫倒在地上
when he rose up his teeth chattered with terror
当他站起来时，他的牙齿因恐惧而颤抖
and he hid behind the couch
他躲在沙发后面
The Emperor leapt to his feet
皇帝跳了起来
he took a lance from a stand and threw it at me
他从架子上拿起一把长枪扔向我
I caught it in its flight
我在它的飞行中抓住了它
I broke the shaft into two pieces
我把轴分成两块
then he shot at me with an arrow
然后他用箭射向我
but I held up my hands as it came to me
但当它来到我面前时，我举起了双手
and I stopped the arrow in mid-air
我把箭停在半空中
Then he drew a dagger from a belt of white leather
然后他从一条白色皮革腰带上抽出一把匕首
and he stabbed the Nubian in the throat
他刺伤了努比亚人的喉咙
so that the the slave would not tell of his dishonour
免得奴仆说出他的耻辱
The man writhed like a trampled snake
那人像一条被践踏的蛇一样扭动着

and a red foam bubbled from his lips
他的嘴唇冒出红色的泡沫
As soon as he was dead the Emperor turned to me
他一死，皇帝就转向我
he took out a little napkin of purple silk
他拿出一张紫色丝绸的小餐巾纸
and he had wiped away the bright sweat from his brow
他擦掉了额头上的汗水
he said to me, "Art thou a prophet?"
他对我说："你是先知吗？"
"is it that I may not harm thee?"
"难道我不能伤害你吗？"
"or are you the son of a prophet?"
"或者你是先知的儿子？"
"and is it that can I do thee no hurt?"
"难道我能不伤害你吗？"
"I pray thee leave my city tonight"
"我祈求你今晚离开我的城市"
"while thou art in my city I am no longer its lord"
"你在我的城里，我不再是城主"
And this time I answered his question
这次我回答了他的问题
"I will leave they city, for half of thy treasure"
"我要离开他们的城，为了你一半的财宝"
"Give me half of thy treasure and I will go away"
"把你一半的财宝给我，我就走了"
"He took me by the hand and led me into the garden"
"他拉着我的手，把我领进了花园"
"When the captain of the guard saw me he wondered"
"当警卫队长看到我时，他想知道"
"When the eunuchs saw me their knees shook"
"太监们看到我，膝盖都颤抖了"
"and they fell upon the ground in fear"
"他们吓得倒在地上"

There is a special chamber in the palace
宫殿里有一个特殊的房间

the chamber has eight walls of red porphyry
房间有八面红色斑岩墙

and it has a brass-scaled ceiling hung with lamps
它有一个黄铜鳞片的天花板，上面挂着灯

The Emperor touched one of the walls and it opened
皇帝摸了摸其中一堵墙，墙开了

we passed down a corridor that was lit with many torches
我们经过一条走廊，走廊上点着许多火把

In niches upon each side stood great wine-jars
在两边的壁龛里放着巨大的酒罐

the wine-jars were filled to the brim with silver pieces
酒罐里装满了银片

soon we reached the centre of the corridor
很快，我们到达了走廊的中心

the Emperor spoke the word that may not be spoken
皇帝说了不能说的话

a granite door swung back on a secret spring
一扇花岗岩门在秘密弹簧上向后摆动

and he put his hands before his face
他把手放在脸前

so that he would not be dazzled
这样他就不会眼花缭乱

Thou would not have believed how marvellous a place it was
你不会相信这是一个多么奇妙的地方

There were huge tortoise-shells full of pearls
有巨大的龟壳，里面装满了珍珠

and there were hollowed moonstones of great size
还有大小不一的空心月光石

the moonstones were piled up with red rubies
月光石上堆满了红色红宝石

The gold was stored in coffers of elephant-hide
黄金被储存在大象皮的金库中

and there was gold-dust in leather bottles
皮瓶里有金粉

There were more opals and sapphires than I could count
蛋白石和蓝宝石多得数不清
the many opals were kept in cups of crystal
许多蛋白石被保存在水晶杯中
and the sapphires were kept in cups of jade
蓝宝石被放在玉杯里
Round green emeralds were arranged in order
圆形绿色祖母绿按顺序排列
they were laid out upon thin plates of ivory
它们被放置在象牙薄板上
in one corner were silk bags full of turquoise-stones
在一个角落里，有装满绿松石的丝绸袋子
and others bags were filled with beryls
其他袋子里装满了绿柱石
The ivory horns were heaped with purple amethysts
象牙角上堆满了紫色的紫水晶
and the horns of brass were heaped with chalcedony and sard stones
黄铜的角上堆满了玉髓和沙德石
The pillars holding the ceiling were made of cedar
支撑天花板的柱子由雪松制成
they were hung with strings of yellow lynx-stones
他们挂着一串串黄色的猞猁石
In the flat oval shields there were carbuncles
在扁平的椭圆形盾牌中有瘤
they were wine-coloured, and coloured like grass
它们是酒色的，颜色像草一样
And yet I have told thee but a fraction of what was there
然而，我告诉你的只是那里的一小部分

The Emperor took away his hands from his face
皇帝把手从脸上移开
he said to me, "this is my house of treasure"
他对我说："这是我的宝藏之家"
half of what is in this house is thine
这房子里有一半是你的
this is as I promised to thee

这是我向你承诺的
And I will give thee camels and camel drivers
我会给你骆驼和骆驼司机
and the camel drivers shall do thy bidding
骆驼车夫必听从你的吩咐
please, take thy share of the treasure
请拿走你的那份宝藏
take it to whatever part of the world thou desirest
把它带到你想要的世界任何地方
But the thing shall be done tonight
但今晚要做这事
because, as you know, the sun is my father
因为，如你所知，太阳是我的父亲
he must not see a man in the city that I cannot slay
他不能在城里看到一个我不能杀的人
But I answered him, "The gold that is here is thine"
但我回答说："这里的金子是你的"
"and the silver that is here also is thine"
"这里的银子也是你的"
"and thine are the precious jewels and opals"
"珍贵的珠宝和蛋白石是你的"
"As for me, I have no need of these treasures"
"至于我，我不需要这些宝藏"
"I shall not take anything from thee"
"我不会从你那里拿走任何东西"
"but I will take the little ring that thou wearest"
"但我要拿走你戴的小戒指"
"it is on the finger of thy hand"
"它在你手的手指上"
when I said this the Emperor frowned
当我说这句话时，皇帝皱起了眉头
"It is but a ring of lead," he cried
"它只不过是一圈铅，"他喊道
"a simple ring has no value for you"
"一枚简单的戒指对你来说毫无价值"
"take thy half of the treasure and go from my city"

- 68 -

"拿走你一半的财宝,离开我的城"
"Nay" I answered, "it is what I want"
"不,"我回答说,"这是我想要的"
"I will take nought but that lead ring"
"除了那个铅环,我什么都不拿"
"for I know what is written within it"
"因为我知道里面写了什么"
"and I know for what purpose it is"
"我知道这是出于什么目的"
And the Emperor trembled in fear
皇帝吓得浑身发抖
he besought me and said, "Take all the treasure"
他恳求我说:"把所有的财宝都拿走"
"take all the treasure and go from my city"
"带走所有的宝藏,离开我的城市"
"The half that is mine shall be thine also"
"属于我的一半也要归你"

And I did a strange thing
我做了一件奇怪的事情
but what I did matters not
但我做了什么并不重要
because there is a cave that is but a day's journey from here
因为有一个山洞,离这里只有一天的路程
in that cave I have hidden the Ring of Riches
在那个山洞里,我藏了一枚财富戒指
in this cave the ring of riches waits for thy coming
在这个山洞里,财富之环等待着你的到来
He who has this Ring is richer than all the kings of the world
拥有这枚戒指的人比世界上所有的国王都富有
Come and take it, and the world's riches shall be thine
来吧,世界的财富将归你所有
But the young Fisherman laughed, "love is better than riches"
但年轻的渔夫笑了,"爱情胜过财富"

"and the little Mermaid loves me," he added
"小美人鱼爱我,"他补充道
"Nay, but there is nothing better than riches," said the Soul
"不,但没有什么比财富更好的了,"灵魂说
"Love is better," answered the young Fisherman
"爱更好,"年轻的渔夫回答
and he plunged back into the deep waters
然后他又跳进了深水区
and the Soul went weeping away over the marshes
灵魂在沼泽地上哭泣

After the Third Year
第三年后

it had been three year since he cast his soul away
自从他抛弃自己的灵魂以来,已经三年了
the Soul came back to the shore of the sea
灵魂回到了海边
and the Soul called to the young Fisherman
灵魂呼唤年轻的渔夫
the young Fisherman rose back out of the sea
年轻的渔夫从海里复活了
he asked his soul, "Why dost thou call me?"
他问他的灵魂:"你为什么叫我?"
And the Soul answered, "Come nearer"
灵魂回答说:"靠近一点"
"come nearer, so that I may speak with thee"
"走近一点,好让我和你说话"
"I have seen marvellous things"
"我见过奇妙的事情"
So the young Fisherman came nearer to his soul
于是,年轻的渔夫更接近他的灵魂
and he couched in the shallow water
他躺在浅水里
and he leaned his head upon his hand
他把头靠在他的手上
and he listened to his Soul
他听从了他的灵魂
and his Soul spoke to him
他的灵魂对他说话

In a city that I know of there is an inn
在我所知道的一个城市里,有一家旅馆
the inn that I speak of stands by a river
我说的客栈矗立在河边
in this inn I sat and drunk with sailors
在这家旅馆里,我和水手们坐在一起喝醉

sailors who drank two different coloured wines
喝两种不同颜色葡萄酒的水手
and they ate bread made of barley
他们吃了大麦做的面包
and I ate salty little fish with them
我和他们一起吃咸咸的小鱼
little fish that were served in bay leaves with vinegar
用月桂叶和醋盛放的小鱼
while we sat and made merry an old man entered
当我们坐着快乐时，一位老人走了进来
he had a leather carpet with him
他随身带着一张皮地毯
and he had a lute that had two horns of amber
他有一把琵琶，上面有两只琥珀角
he laid out the carpet on the floor
他把地毯铺在地板上
and he struck on the strings of his lute
他敲击着琵琶的琴弦
and a girl ran in and began to dance in front of us
一个女孩跑进来，开始在我们面前跳舞
Her face was veiled with a veil of gauze
她的脸上蒙着纱布
and she was wearing silk, but her feet were naked
她穿着丝绸，但她的脚是赤裸的
and her feet moved over the carpet like little white pigeons
她的脚像小白鸽一样在地毯上移动
Never have I seen anything so marvellous
我从未见过如此奇妙的东西
the city where she dances is but a day's journey from here
她跳舞的城市距离这里只有一天的路程
the young Fisherman heard the words of his Soul
年轻的渔夫听到了他灵魂的话
he remembered that the little Mermaid had no feet
他记得小美人鱼没有脚
and he remembered she was unable to dance
他记得她不能跳舞

a great desire came over him to see the girl
他强烈渴望见到这个女孩
he said to himself, "It is but a day's journey"
他对自己说:"这只是一天的旅程"
"and then I can return to my love," he laughed
"然后我就可以回到我的爱人身边了,"他笑着说
he stood up in the shallow water
他在浅水区站了起来
and he strode towards the shore
他大步向岸边走去
when he had reached the dry shore he laughed again
当他到达干涸的岸边时,他又笑了
and he held out his arms to his Soul
他向他的灵魂伸出双臂
his Soul gave a great cry of joy
他的灵魂发出了巨大的喜悦呼喊
his Soul ran to meet his body
他的灵魂跑去迎接他的身体
and his Soul entered into back him again
他的灵魂又进入了他
the young Fisherman became one with his shadow once more
年轻的渔夫再次与他的影子合而为一
the shadow of the body that is the body of the Soul
身体的影子,即灵魂的身体
And his Soul said to him, "Let us not tarry"
他的灵魂对他说:"让我们不要拖延"
"but let us get going at once"
"但是让我们马上开始吧"
"because the Sea-gods are jealous"
"因为海神嫉妒"
"and they have monsters that do their bidding"
"他们有听命于他们的怪物"
So they made haste to get to the city
于是他们匆匆忙忙地赶到城里

Sin
罪

all that night they journeyed beneath the moon
那天晚上,他们在月亮下旅行
and all the next day they journeyed beneath the sun
第二天,他们在太阳底下旅行
on the evening of the day they came to a city
当天傍晚,他们来到一座城市
the young Fisherman asked his Soul
年轻的渔夫问他的灵魂
"Is this the city in which she dances?"
"这是她跳舞的城市吗?"
And his Soul answered him
他的灵魂回答了他
"It is not this city, but another"
"不是这个城市,而是另一个城市"
"Nevertheless, let us enter this city"
"不过,让我们进入这个城市"
So they entered the city and passed through the streets
于是他们进了城,穿过街道
they passed through the street of jewellers
他们穿过珠宝商的街道
passing through the street, the young Fisherman saw a silver cup
穿过街道,年轻的渔夫看到一个银杯
his Soul said to him, "Take that silver cup"
他的灵魂对他说:"拿着那个银杯"
and his Soul told him to hide the silver cup
他的灵魂告诉他要把银杯藏起来
So he took the silver cup and hid it
于是他拿起银杯,把它藏了起来
and they went hurriedly out of the city
他们匆匆忙忙地出了城
the young Fisherman frowned and flung the cup away
年轻的渔夫皱起眉头,把杯子甩开了

"Why did'st thou tell me to take this cup?"
"你为什么不叫我拿这个杯子？"
"it was an evil thing to do"
"这是一件邪恶的事情"
But his Soul just told him to be at peace
但他的灵魂只是告诉他要平静

on the evening of the second day they came to a city
第二天傍晚，他们来到了一座城市
the young Fisherman asked his Soul
年轻的渔夫问他的灵魂
"Is this the city in which she dances?"
"这是她跳舞的城市吗？"
And his Soul answered him
他的灵魂回答了他
"It is not this city, but another"
"不是这个城市，而是另一个城市"
"Nevertheless, let us enter this city"
"不过，让我们进入这个城市"
So they entered in and passed through the streets
于是他们进去，穿过街道
they passed through the street of sandal sellers
他们穿过凉鞋卖家的街道
passing through the street, the young Fisherman saw a child
路过街道，年轻的渔夫看到一个孩子
the child was standing by a jar of water
孩子站在一罐水旁边
his Soul told him to smite the child
他的灵魂告诉他要打孩子
So he smote the child till it wept
于是他打孩子，直到孩子哭泣
after he had done this they went hurriedly out of the city
他做完这些后，他们匆匆忙忙地出了城
the young Fisherman grew angry with his soul
年轻的渔夫对他的灵魂感到愤怒
"Why did'st thou tell me to smite the child?"

"你为什么不叫我打孩子？"
"it was an evil thing to do"
"这是一件邪恶的事情"
But his Soul just told him to be at peace
但他的灵魂只是告诉他要平静

And on the evening of the third day they came to a city
第三天傍晚，他们来到一座城市
the young Fisherman asked his Soul
年轻的渔夫问他的灵魂
"Is this the city in which she dances?"
"这是她跳舞的城市吗？"
And his Soul answered him
他的灵魂回答了他
"It may be that it is this city, so let us enter"
"可能是这个城市，所以让我们进去"
So they entered the city and passed through the streets
于是他们进了城，穿过街道
but nowhere could the young Fisherman find the river
但年轻的渔夫却无处可寻
and he couldn't find the inn either
他也找不到客栈
And the people of the city looked curiously at him
城里的人都好奇地看着他
and he grew afraid and asked his Soul to leave
他害怕了，要求他的灵魂离开
"she who dances with white feet is not here"
"白脚舞的她不在这里"
But his Soul answered "Nay, but let us rest"
但他的灵魂回答说："不，但让我们休息吧"
"because the night is dark"
"因为夜很黑"
"and there will be robbers on the way"
"路上会有强盗"
So he sat himself down in the market-place and rested
于是，他坐在集市上休息

after a time a hooded merchant walked past him
过了一会儿，一个戴着兜帽的商人从他身边走过
he had a cloak of cloth of Tartary
他有一件鞑靼的布斗篷
and he carried a lantern of pierced horn
他提着一盏穿孔的角灯笼
the merchant asked the young Fisherman
商人问年轻的渔夫
"Why dost thou sit in the market-place?"
"你为什么坐在集市上？"
"the booths are closed and the bales corded"
"摊位关闭了，捆包被绑起来了"
And the young Fisherman answered him
年轻的渔夫回答了他
"I can find no inn in this city"
"我在这个城市找不到旅馆"
"I have no kinsman who might give me shelter"
"我没有亲戚可以给我庇护"
"Are we not all kinsmen?" said the merchant
"我们不都是亲戚吗？"商人说
"And did not one God make us?"
"难道不是一位上帝创造了我们吗？"
"come with me, for I have a guest-chamber"
"跟我来，因为我有一个客房"
So the young Fisherman rose up and followed the merchant
于是，年轻的渔夫站了起来，跟着商人走了
they passed through a garden of pomegranates
他们穿过一个石榴园
and they entered into the house of the merchant
他们进了商人的家
the merchant brought him rose-water in a copper dish
商人给他端来了装在铜盘子里的玫瑰水
so that he could wash his hands
这样他就可以洗手了
and he brought him ripe melons
他给他带来了成熟的瓜

so that he could quench his thirst
这样他就可以解渴了

and he gave him a bowl of rice
他给了他一碗米饭

in the bowl of rice was roasted lamb
一碗米饭里是烤羊肉

so that he could satisfy his hunger
这样他就可以满足他的饥饿感

the young Fischerman finished his meal
年轻的费舍尔曼吃完了饭

and he thanked the merchant for all his generousity
他感谢商人的慷慨解囊

then the merchant led him to the guest-chamber
然后商人把他带到了客房

and the merchant let him sleep in his chamber
商人让他睡在他的房间里

the young Fisherman gave him thanks again
年轻的渔夫再次向他表示感谢

and he kissed the ring that was on his hand
他吻了吻他手上的戒指

he flung himself down on the carpets of dyed goat's-hair
他扑倒在染了山羊毛的地毯上

And when pulled the blanket over himself he fell asleep
当把毯子盖在自己身上时，他睡着了

it was three hours before dawn
距离黎明还有三个小时

while it was still night his Soul woke him
趁着夜色，他的灵魂唤醒了他

his Soul told him to rise
他的灵魂告诉他要复活

"Rise up and go to the room of the merchant"
"起来，去商人的房间"

"go to the room in which he sleeps"
"去他睡觉的房间"

"slay him in his sleep"

"在他睡梦中杀了他"
"take his gold from him"
"从他那里拿走他的金子"
"because we have need of it"
"因为我们需要它"
And the young Fisherman rose up
年轻的渔夫站了起来
and he crept towards the room of the merchant
他蹑手蹑脚地走向商人的房间
there was a curved sword at the feet of the merchant
商人脚下有一把弯曲的剑
and there was a tray by the side of the merchant
商人旁边有一个托盘
the tray held nine purses of gold
托盘里装着九个金钱包
And he reached out his hand and touched the sword
他伸出手去摸那把剑
and when he touched the sword the merchant woke up
当他碰到剑时，商人醒了过来
he leapt up and seized the sword
他跳了起来，抓住了剑
"Dost thou return evil for good?"
"你以恶报善吗？"
"do you pay with the shedding of blood?"
"你以流血为代价吗？"
"in return for the kindness that I have shown thee"
"为了报答我对你的好意"
And his Soul said to the young Fisherman, "Strike him"
他的灵魂对年轻的渔夫说："打他"
and he struck him so that he swooned
他打了他，使他昏迷了
he seized the nine purses of gold
他抓住了九个金袋
and he fled hastily through the garden of pomegranates
他匆匆忙忙地逃过石榴园
and he set his face to the star of morning

他把脸对准晨星

they escaped the city without being noticed
他们在没有被发现的情况下逃离了这座城市

the young Fisherman beat his breast
年轻的渔夫捶胸顿足

"Why didst thou bid me to slay the merchant?"
"你为什么要叫我杀了商人？"

"why did you make me take his gold?"
"你为什么要让我拿走他的金子？"

"Surely thou art evil"
"你肯定是邪恶的"

But his Soul told him to be at peace
但他的灵魂告诉他要平安

"No!" cried the young Fisherman
"不！"年轻的渔夫喊道

"I can not be at peace with this"
"我无法对此感到平静"

"all that thou hast made me do I hate"
"你使我所做的一切，我都恨不入"

"and what else I hate is you"
"我还讨厌你"

"why have you brought me here to do these things?"
"你为什么把我带到这里来做这些事情？"

And his Soul answered him
他的灵魂回答了他

"When you sent me into the world you gave me no heart"
"当你把我送到世界上时，你没有给我心"

"so I learned to do all these things"
"所以我学会了做所有这些事情"

"and I learned to love these things"
"我学会了爱这些东西"

"What sayest thou?" murmured the young Fisherman
"你说什么？"年轻的渔夫喃喃自语

"Thou knowest," answered his Soul
"你知道，"他的灵魂回答

"Have you forgotten that you gave me no heart?"

"你忘了你没有给我心吗?"
"don't trouble yourself for me, but be at peace"
"不要为我找麻烦,但要平安"
"because there is no pain you shouldn't give away"
"因为没有痛苦,你不应该放弃"
"and there is no pleasure that you should not receive"
"没有什么快乐是你不应该得到的"
when the young Fisherman heard these words he trembled
年轻的渔夫听到这句话,浑身发抖
"Nay, but thou art evil"
"不,但你是邪恶的"
"you have made me forget my love"
"你让我忘记了我的爱"
"you have tempted me with temptations"
"你用试探试探我"
"and you have set my feet in the ways of sin"
"你使我踏上了罪恶的道路"
And his Soul answered him
他的灵魂回答了他
"you have not forgotten?"
"你没忘了吗?"
"you sent me into the world with no heart"
"你把我送到这个世界上,没有心"
"Come, let us go to another city"
"来吧,我们去另一个城市"
"let us make merry with the gold we have"
"让我们用我们拥有的黄金来快乐"
But the young Fisherman took the nine purses of gold
但年轻的渔夫拿走了九个金钱包
he flung the purses of gold into the sand
他把装着金子的钱包扔进沙子里
and he trampled on the on the purses of gold
他踩在金子的钱包上
"Nay!" he cried to his Soul
"不!"他向他的灵魂喊道
"I will have nought to do with thee"

"我不会和你有任何关系"
"I will not journey with thee anywhere"
"我不会和你一起去任何地方"
"I have sent thee away before"
"我以前把你送走了"
"and I will send thee away again"
"我再打发你走"
"because thou hast brought me no good"
"因为你没有给我带来任何好处"
And he turned his back to the moon
他背对着月亮
he held the little green knife in his hand
他手里拿着那把绿色的小刀
he strove to cut from his feet the shadow of the body
他努力从脚上剪下身体的影子
the shadow of the body, which is the body of the Soul
身体的影子，也就是灵魂的身体
Yet his Soul stirred not from him
然而，他的灵魂并没有从他身上激起
and it paid no heed to his command
它不听他的命令
"The spell the Witch told thee avails no more"
"女巫告诉你的咒语已经无用了"
"I may not leave thee anymore"
"我可能不会再离开你了"
"and thou can't drive me forth"
"你不能把我赶出去"
"Once in his life may a man send his Soul away"
"一个人一生中只有一次可以把他的灵魂送走"
"but he who receives back his Soul must keep it for ever"
"但谁领回了他的灵魂，就必须永远保守它"
"this is his punishment and his reward"
"这是他的惩罚，也是他的奖赏"
the young Fisherman grew pale at his fate
年轻的渔夫对自己的命运感到苍白
and he clenched his hands and cried

他紧握双手哭泣
"She was a false Witch for not telling me"
"她是个假女巫,因为她没有告诉我"
"Nay," answered his Soul, "she was not a false Witch"
"不,"他的灵魂回答说,"她不是假女巫"
"but she was true to Him she worships"
"但她对他忠心耿耿,她崇拜"
"and she will be his servant forever"
"她将永远是他的仆人"
the young Fisherman knew he could not get rid of his Soul again
年轻的渔夫知道他再也无法摆脱他的灵魂了
he knew now that his soul was an evil Soul
他现在知道他的灵魂是一个邪恶的灵魂
and his Soul would abide with him always
他的灵魂将永远与他同在
when he knew this he fell upon the ground and wept
当他知道这一点时,他倒在地上哭泣

The Heart
心

when it was day the young Fisherman rose up
天亮时，年轻的渔夫站了起来
he told his Soul, "I will bind my hands"
他告诉他的灵魂，"我会束缚我的双手"
"that way I can not do thy bidding"
"这样我就不能听从你的吩咐了"
"and I will close my lips"
"我会闭上嘴唇"
"that way I can not speak thy words"
"这样我就不能说你的话了"
"and I will return to the place where my love lives"
"我会回到我爱人居住的地方"
"to the sea will I return"
"我会回到大海"
"I will return to where she sung to me"
"我会回到她唱歌给我听的地方"
"and I will call to her"
"我会呼唤她"
"I will tell her the evil I have done"
"我会告诉她我所做的恶"
"and I will tell her the evil thou hast wrought on me"
"我要告诉她你对我造成的恶"
his Soul tempted him, "Who is thy love?"
他的灵魂试探他，"你的爱人是谁？"
"why should thou return to her?"
"你为什么要回到她身边？"
"The world has many fairer than she is"
"世界上有很多比她更公平的"
"There are the dancing-girls of Samaris"
"有撒玛利亚的舞女"
"they dance the way birds dance"
"他们像鸟儿跳舞一样跳舞"
"and they dance the way beasts dance"

"他们像野兽跳舞一样跳舞"
"Their feet are painted with henna"
"他们的脚上涂满了指甲花"
"in their hands they have little copper bells"
"他们手里拿着小铜铃"
"They laugh while they dance"
"他们一边跳舞一边笑"
"their laughter is as clear as the laughter of water"
"他们的笑声像水的笑声一样清晰"
"Come with me and I will show them to thee"
"跟我来,我给你看"
"because why trouble yourself with things of sin?"
"因为为什么要为罪事烦恼呢?"
"Is that which is pleasant to eat not made to be eaten?"
"吃起来好吃的,难道不是用来吃的吗?"
"Is there poison in that which is sweet to drink?"
"喝甜的东西里有毒吗?"
"Trouble not thyself, but come with me to another city"
"不要给自己找麻烦,跟我去另一个城市"
"There is a little city with a garden of tulip-trees"
"有一个小城市,有一个郁金香树花园"
"in its garden there are white peacocks"
"在它的花园里有白孔雀"
"and there are peacocks that have blue breasts"
"还有蓝胸的孔雀"
"Their tails are like disks of ivory"
"它们的尾巴就像象牙的圆盘"
"when they spread their tails in the sun"
"当他们在阳光下张开尾巴时"
"And she who feeds them dances for their pleasure"
"喂他们吃饭的人跳舞是为了他们的快乐"
"and sometimes she dances on her hands"
"有时她会用手跳舞"
"and at other times she dances with her feet"
"在其他时候,她用脚跳舞"
"Her eyes are coloured with stibium"

"她的眼睛是用锑着色的"

"her nostrils are shaped like the wings of a swallow"
"她的鼻孔形状像燕子的翅膀"

"and she laughs while she dances"
"她跳舞时会笑"

"and the silver rings on her ankles ring"
"还有她脚踝上的银戒指"

"Don't trouble thyself any more"
"不要再给自己找麻烦了"

"come with me to this city"
"跟我来这个城市"

But the young Fisherman did not answer his Soul
但年轻的渔夫没有回答他的灵魂

he closed his lips with the seal of silence
他用沉默的封印闭上了嘴唇

and he bound his own hands with a tight cord
他用一根紧绷的绳子绑住自己的双手

and he journeyed back to from where he had come
于是他又回到了他来时的地方

he journeyd back to the little bay
他回到了小海湾

and he journeyed to where his love had sung for him
他走到他的爱为他歌唱的地方

His Soul tried to tempt him along the way
他的灵魂一路上试图诱惑他

but he made his Soul no answer
但他使他的灵魂没有回答

and he did none of his Soul's wickedness
他没有做他灵魂的邪恶

so great was the power of the love that was within him
他内在的爱的力量是如此之大

when he reached the shore he loosened the cord
当他到达岸边时,他松开了绳子

and he took the seal of silence from his lips
他从嘴唇上取下了沉默的印记

he called out to the little Mermaid
他呼唤着小美人鱼
But she did not answer his call for her
但她没有回应他对她的呼唤
she did not answer, although he called all day
她没有接,尽管他整天都在打电话
his Soul mocked the young Fisherman
他的灵魂嘲笑年轻的渔夫
"you have little joy out of thy love"
"你从你的爱中得不到什么喜乐"
"you are pouring water into a broken vessel"
"你正在把水倒进一个破损的容器里"
"you have given away what you had"
"你已经放弃了你所拥有的"
"but nothing has been given to you in return"
"但什么也没给你"
"It would be better if you came with me"
"如果你跟我一起去会更好"
"because I know where the Valley of Pleasure lies"
"因为我知道快乐之谷在哪里"
But the young Fisherman did not answer his Soul
但年轻的渔夫没有回答他的灵魂

in a cleft of the rock he built himself a house
在岩石的裂缝里,他给自己盖了一座房子
and he abode there for the space of a year
他在那里住了一年
every morning he called to the Mermaid
每天早上,他都会呼唤美人鱼
and every noon he called to her again
每天中午,他又叫她
and at night-time he spoke her name
到了晚上,他才说出她的名字
but she never rose out of the sea to meet him
但她从未从海里升起迎接他
and he could not find her anywhere in the sea

他在海里的任何地方都找不到她
he sought for her in the caves
他在山洞里寻找她
he sought for her in the green water
他在绿水中寻找她
he sought for her in the pools of the tide
他在潮汐的潭中寻找她
and he sought for her in the wells
他在井里寻找她
the wells that are at the bottom of the deep
深海底部的井
his Soul didn't stop tempting him with evil
他的灵魂并没有停止用邪恶诱惑他
and it whispered terrible things to him
它向他低声说着可怕的事情
but his Soul could not prevail against him
但他的灵魂无法战胜他
the power of his love was too great
他的爱的力量太大了

after the year was over the Soul thought within itself
一年过后,灵魂在自己内部思考
"I have tempted my master with evil"
"我用邪恶诱惑了我的主人"
"but his love is stronger than I am"
"但他的爱比我强"
"I will tempt him now with good"
"我现在要用好东西诱惑他"
"it may be that he will come with me"
"也许他会和我一起去"
So he spoke to the young Fisherman
于是他对年轻的渔夫说了一句话
"I have told thee of the joy of the world"
"我已将世人的喜乐告诉过你"
"and thou hast turned a deaf ear to me"
"你对我充耳不闻"

- 88 -

"allow me to tell thee of the world's pain"
"请允许我告诉你世界的痛苦"
"and it may be that you will listen"
"也许你会听的"
"because pain is the Lord of this world"
"因为痛苦是这个世界的主"
"and there is no one who escapes from its net"
"没有人能逃脱它的网"
"There be some who lack raiment"
"有些人缺乏衣物"
"and there are others who lack bread"
"还有一些人缺面包"
"There are widows who sit in purple"
"有穿着紫色衣服的寡妇"
"and there are widows who sit in rags"
"还有衣衫褴褛的寡妇"
"The beggars go up and down on the roads"
"乞丐在路上上上下下"
"and the pockets of the beggars are empty"
"乞丐的口袋是空的"
"Through the streets of the cities walks famine"
"穿过城市的街道,走过饥荒"
"and the plague sits at their gates"
"瘟疫就在他们的门口"
"Come, let us go forth and mend these things"
"来吧,我们出去修补这些东西"
"let us make these things be different"
"让我们让这些事情变得不同"
"why should you wait here calling to thy love?"
"你为什么要在这里等待呼唤你的爱?"
"she will not come to your call"
"她不会来接你的电话的"
"And what is love?"
"什么是爱?"
"And why do you value it so highly?"
"你为什么这么看重它?"

But the young Fisherman didn't answer his Soul
但年轻的渔夫没有回答他的灵魂

so great was the power of his love
他的爱的力量是如此之大

And every morning he called to the Mermaid
每天早上，他都会呼唤美人鱼

and every noon he called to her again
每天中午，他又叫她

and at night-time he spoke her name
到了晚上，他才说出她的名字

Yet never did she rise out of the sea to meet him
然而，她从未从海中升起与他相遇

nor in any place of the sea could he find her
他在海的任何地方也找不到她

though he sought for her in the rivers of the sea
虽然他在海的河流中寻找她

and in the valleys that are under the waves
在海浪下的山谷中

in the sea that the night makes purple
在黑夜使紫色的大海中

and in the sea that the dawn leaves grey
在黎明离开灰色的大海中

after the second year was over
第二年结束后

the Soul spoke to the young Fisherman at night-time
灵魂在夜间对年轻的渔夫说话

while he sat in the wattled house alone
当他独自坐在瓦特的房子里时

"I have tempted thee with evil"
"我用邪恶试探你"

"and I have tempted thee with good"
"我用善试探你"

"and thy love is stronger than I am"
"你的爱比我更坚强"

"I will tempt thee no longer"
"我不会再试探你了"

"but please, allow me to enter thy heart"
"但请允许我进入你的心"
"so that I may be one with thee, as before"
"使我能像以前一样与你合而为一"
"thou mayest enter," said the young Fisherman
"你可以进去了,"年轻的渔夫说
"because when you had no heart you must have suffered"
"因为当你没有心的时候,你一定受苦了"
"Alas!" cried his Soul
"唉!"他的灵魂喊道
"I can find no place of entrance"
"我找不到入口"
"so compassed about with love is this heart of thine"
"你的这颗心被爱所包围"
"I wish that I could help thee," said the young Fisherman
"我希望我能帮你,"年轻的渔夫说
while he spoke there came a great cry of mourning from the sea
当他说话时,海里传来了一声巨大的哀悼声
the cry that men hear when one of the Sea-folk is dead
当一个海民死去时,人们听到的哭声
the young Fisherman leapt up and left his house
年轻的渔夫跳起来离开了他的房子
and he ran down to the shore
他跑到岸边
the black waves came hurrying to the shore
黑色的海浪匆匆忙忙地向岸边袭来
the waves carried a burden that was whiter than silver
海浪承载着比银子还白的包袱
it was as white as the surf
它像海浪一样洁白
and it tossed on the waves like a flower
它像一朵花一样在海浪上翻腾
And the surf took it from the waves
海浪把它从海浪中带走了
and the foam took it from the surf

泡沫从海浪中带走了它
and the shore received it
岸边收到了它
lying at his feet was the body of the little Mermaid
躺在他脚下的是小美人鱼的尸体
She was lying dead at his feet
她躺在他脚边死了
he flung himself beside her, and wept
他扑倒在她身边，哭了起来
he kissed the cold red of her mouth
他吻了吻她嘴角冰冷的红色
and he stroked the wet amber of her hair
他抚摸着她湿漉漉的琥珀色头发
he wept like someone trembling with joy
他哭了，就像一个喜极而颤抖的人
in his brown arms he held her to his breast
在他棕色的怀抱里，他把她抱在胸前
Cold were the lips, yet he kissed them
嘴唇很冷，但他吻了它们
salty was the honey of her hair
咸是她头发的蜂蜜
yet he tasted it with a bitter joy
然而，他却带着苦涩的喜悦品尝了它
He kissed her closed eyelids
他吻了她紧闭的眼皮
the wild spray that lay upon her was less salty than his tears
洒在她身上的狂野喷雾比他的眼泪还咸
to the dead little mermaid he made a confession
他向死去的小美人鱼坦白了
Into the shells of her ears he poured the harsh wine of his tale
他把他故事中的烈酒倒进她的耳朵里
He put the little hands round his neck
他把小手放在他的脖子上
and with his fingers he touched the thin reed of her throat
他用手指摸了摸她喉咙里细细的芦苇

his joy was bitter and deep
他的喜悦是苦涩而深沉的
and his pain was full of a strange gladness
他的痛苦充满了一种奇怪的喜悦
The black sea came nearer
黑海越来越近了
and the white foam moaned like a leper
白色的泡沫像麻风病人一样呻吟
the sea grabbed at the shore with its white claws of foam
大海用白色的泡沫爪子抓住岸边
From the palace of the Sea-King came the cry of mourning again
从海王的宫殿里又传来了哀悼的呼喊声
far out upon the sea the great Tritons could be heard
在遥远的海面上，可以听到巨大的特里顿
they blew hoarsely upon their horns
他们嘶哑地吹着喇叭
"Flee away," said his Soul
"逃走，"他的灵魂说
"if the sea comes nearer it will slay thee"
"如果大海靠近它，它会杀死你"
"please, let us leave, for I am afraid"
"求求你，让我们离开吧，因为我害怕"
"because thy heart is closed against me"
"因为你的心对我封闭"
"out of the greatness of thy love I beg you
"出于你伟大的爱，我恳求你
"flee away to a place of safety"
"逃到安全的地方"
"Surely you would not do this to me again?"
"你肯定不会再这样对我了吗？"
"do not send me into another world without a heart"
"不要把我送进另一个没有心的世界"
the young Fisherman did not listen to his Soul
年轻的渔夫没有听从他的灵魂
but he spole to the little Mermaid

但他向小美人鱼嘶吼

and he said, "Love is better than wisdom"

他说,"爱胜于智慧"

"love is more precious than riches"

"爱情比财富更宝贵"

"love fairer than the feet of the daughters of men"

"爱比男人女儿的脚更公平"

"The fires of the world cannot destroy love"

"世界的火焰不能摧毁爱情"

"the waters of the sea cannot quench love"

"海水不能熄灭爱"

"I called on thee at dawn"

"我在黎明时分呼唤你"

"and thou didst not come to my call"

"你没有听从我的呼召"

"The moon heard thy name"

"月亮听见了你的名字"

"but the moon didn't answer me"

"可是月亮没有回答我"

"I left thee in order to do evil"

"我离开你是为了作恶"

"and I have suffered for what I've done"

"我为我的所作所为受苦"

"but my love for you has never left me"

"但我对你的爱从未离开过我"

"and my love was always strong"

"我的爱总是很强烈"

"nothing prevailed against my love"

"没有什么能战胜我的爱"

"though I have looked upon evil"

"虽然我看见了邪恶"

"and I have looked upon good"

"我看好了"

"now that thou are dead, I will also die with thee"

"既然你死了,我也要和你一起死"

his Soul begged him to depart

他的灵魂恳求他离开
but he would not leave, so great was his love
但他不肯离开,他的爱是如此之大
the sea came nearer to the shore
大海离岸边越来越近了
and the sea sought to cover him with its waves
大海试图用波浪覆盖他
the young Fisherman knew that the end was at hand
年轻的渔夫知道末日就在眼前
he kissed the cold lips of the Mermaid
他吻了吻美人鱼冰冷的嘴唇
and the heart that was within him broke
他内心的心碎了
from the fullness of his love his heart did break
从他满满的爱中,他的心确实破碎了
the Soul found an entrance, and entered his heart
灵魂找到了入口,进入了他的心
his Soul was one with him, just like before
他的灵魂与他合而为一,就像以前一样
And the sea covered the young Fisherman with its waves
大海用波浪覆盖了年轻的渔夫

Blessings
祝福

in the morning the Priest went forth to bless the sea
早上，祭司出去祝福大海
because the Priest had been troubled that night
因为那天晚上神父很烦恼
the monks and the musicians went with him
僧侣和音乐家和他一起去
and the candle-bearers came with the Priest too
持烛的人也和祭司一起来了
and the swingers of censers came with the Priest
香炉的浪荡公子和牧师一起来了
and a great company of people followed him
一大群人跟着他
when the Priest reached the shore he saw the young Fisherman
当牧师到达岸边时，他看到了年轻的渔夫
he was lying drowned in the surf
他躺在海浪中淹死了
clasped in his arms was the body of the little Mermaid
他怀里抱着小美人鱼的尸体
And the Priest drew back frowning
牧师皱着眉头往后退
he made the sign of the cross and exclaimed aloud:
他做了十字架的记号，大声喊道：
"I will not bless the sea, nor anything that is in it"
"我不会祝福大海，也不会祝福其中的任何东西"
"Accursed be the Sea-folk and those who traffic with them"
"海民和与他们一起交易的人被诅咒"
"And as for the young Fisherman;"
"至于年轻的渔夫；"
"he forsook God for the sake of love"
"他为爱的缘故抛弃了上帝"
"and now he lays here with his lover"
"现在他和他的爱人躺在这里"

"he was slain by God's judgement"
"他被上帝的审判杀死了"
"take up his body and the body of his lover"
"拿起他的身体和他爱人的身体"
"bury them in the corner of the Field"
"把他们埋在田野的角落里"
"let no mark of why they were be set above them"
"不要记下他们为什么被置于他们之上"
"don't give them any sign of any kind"
"不要给他们任何迹象"
"none shall know the place of their resting"
"没有人知道他们安息的地方"
"because they were accursed in their lives"
"因为他们在生活中被诅咒"
"and they shall be accursed in their deaths"
"他们死必受咒诅"
And the people did as he commanded them
百姓就照他的吩咐去做
in the corner of the field where no sweet herbs grew
在田野的角落里，没有甜草生长
they dug a deep pit for their graves
他们为自己的坟墓挖了一个深坑
and they laid the dead things within the pit
他们把死物放在坑里

when the third year was over
第三年结束时
on a day that was a holy day
在那一天，那是一个神圣的日子
the Priest went up to the chapel
神父走到教堂里
he went to show the people the wounds of the Lord
他去向百姓展示主的伤口
and he spoke to them about the wrath of God
他向他们讲述了神的忿怒
he bowed himself before the altar

他在祭坛前鞠躬
he saw the altar was covered with strange flowers
他看到祭坛上开满了奇怪的花朵
flowers that he had never seen before
他从未见过的花朵
they were strange to look at
他们看起来很奇怪
but they had an interesting kind beauty
但他们有一种有趣的善良美
their beauty troubled him in a strange way
他们的美丽以一种奇怪的方式困扰着他
their odour was sweet in his nostrils
它们的气味在他的鼻孔里很甜
he felt glad, but he did not understand why
他感到高兴，但他不明白为什么
he began to speak to the people
他开始对人们说话
he wanted to speak to them about the wrath of God
他想向他们讲述神的忿怒
but the beauty of the white flowers troubled him
但白花的美丽使他感到不安
and their odour was sweet in his nostrils
他们的气味在他的鼻孔里是甜的
and another word came onto his lip
又说了一句话
he did not speak about the wrath of God
他没有谈到神的忿怒
but he spoke of the God whose name is Love
但他说的是那位名叫爱的神
he did not know why he spoke of this
他不知道他为什么说这个
when he had finished the people wept
当他完成时，人们哭了
the Priest went back to the sacristy
神父回到圣器收藏室
and his eyes too were full of tears

他的眼睛里也充满了泪水

the deacons came in and began to unrobe him
执事们进来，开始给他脱衣服

And he stood as if he was in a dream
他站在那里，仿佛在梦中

"What are the flowers that stand on the altar?"
"祭坛上矗立的花是什么？"

"where did they come from?"
"他们从哪里来？"

And they answered him
他们回答了他

"What flowers they are we cannot tell"
"它们是什么花，我们说不清"

"but they come from the corner of the field"
"但他们来自田野的角落"

the Priest trembled at what he heard
牧师听到的话吓得浑身发抖

and he returned to his house and prayed
他回到家里祷告

in the morning, while it was still dawn
早上，天还没亮

the priest went forth with the monks
牧师和僧侣们一起出去了

he went forth with the musicians
他和音乐家们一起出去了

the candle-bearers and the swingers of censers
蜡烛的持有者和香炉的摆动者

and he had a great company of people
他有一大群人

and he came to the shore of the sea
他来到了海边

he showed them how he blessed the sea
他向他们展示了他如何祝福大海

and he blessed all the wild things that are in it
他祝福了里面所有的野物

he also blessed the fauns
他还祝福了牧神
and he blessed the little things that dance in the woodland
他祝福那些在林地里跳舞的小东西
and he blessed the bright-eyed things that peer through the leaves
他祝福那些透过树叶窥视的明亮眼睛的东西
he blessed all the things in God's world
他祝福了上帝世界里的一切
and the people were filled with joy and wonder
百姓都充满了喜悦和惊奇
but flowers never grew again in the corner of the field
但田野的角落里再也没有开过花
and the Sea-folk never came into the bay again
海民再也没有进入海湾
because they had gone to another part of the sea
因为他们去了海的另一部分

The End
结束

www.ingramcontent.com/pod-product-compliance
Lightning Source LLC
Chambersburg PA
CBHW011953090526
44591CB00020B/2746